Upgrade Your Life! Your Blueprint for Success

By Lorne Lee, Ed.D.

© 2024 Inner Sound Books

A CIP record for this book is available from the Library of Congress Cataloging-in-Publication Data

ISBN-10: 0 98016 149 5

ISBN-13: 978 0 9801614 9 6

Printed in USA

Lorne Lee, Ed.D.

UPGRADE YOUR LIFE!
YOUR BLUEPRINT FOR SUCCESS

Inner Sound Books

Upgrade Your Life!

Your Blueprint for Success

Lorne Lee, E.d.D.

I am grateful to my beloved wife, Amanda, and my parents, H. David Lee and Betty Lee for their unconditional love and support, my sister, Lorriana, and all my siblings for their encouragement, and finally, my extended family and friends, whose belief in me made this book possible.

Table of Contents

Meet the Author
Lorne Lee, Ed.D.

Dr. Lorne Lee is an educator, speaker, musician, and academic advisor who has worked as a professor, summer school director, band director, instructional designer, academic advisor, and Chair of General Studies at nine colleges. He has a Bachelor of Music from the University of Central Oklahoma, a Master of Music from Howard University, and a Doctor of Education from Governors State University.

Dr. Lee is a re-educator. He specializes in empowering people through goals-based systems and sight-shifting. Dr. Lee doesn't just motivate people. He shows them how to create a system so they can become the key to their success. Dr. Lee believes anyone can achieve their goals with a plan and the right motivation. He inspires people to take action with his powerful Upgrade Your Life system. His mission is to empower people to become the solution to their problems and the key to their success.

High school students and early college students are all facing one major fear. What comes next? There is a lot of hope and excitement about what comes next, but the fear is very real. There is even more fear for the parents. And then, there is more fear for school administrators because they need to know if their students will succeed after graduation. It is all about what comes next, and this book teaches you how to build a system around what

1

is next. Systems work better than hope. Everybody hopes, but not everyone has a system that gives them the power to reach their goals. So, *Upgrade Your Life* and join the high achievers of life!

CHAPTER ONE

Having Trouble Unlocking the Door to Success?

What you want, you must first become!

Have you ever felt like your dreams were behind a locked door, only to figure out you do not have the right key? It feels so frustrating, and frustration can lead to anger. If you have ever felt like that, this book is for you. Reaching your goals is about having the right key to the right door, which is you. If you try to achieve your goals without becoming the key that opens the door, you will either quit or break the key and feel hurt by the disappointment. However, you can have your dreams and win the game of life if you can become the key to your success.

We all come to this life with an automatic goal-seeking system. This system takes whatever we focus on the most and pushes us towards it. It is like this big machine in our heads activates and then uses our thoughts as GPS coordinates to drive us toward what we focus on the most. Our job is to take control of this automatic goal-seeking system and use this power to accomplish our goals. This book is the blueprint for taking control of that system.

Upgrade Your Life will show you how to become the key to unlocking the doors to your goals. You do not have to be a genius to start. You don't even need confidence. You have what it takes because you were born with it. You were born with a system that allows you to think, feel, and grow. You might be surprised that very few people have a system for getting what they want. The people who develop winning systems become known as sports champions, business leaders, and government officials. Sometimes, people get lucky, but being lucky means you don't know when it will happen, so you can't depend on it.

What if you can become a champion or leader by building a goal-based success system? Reaching goals is not about being smart. It is about having a system for achieving them and being consistent. You can win if you develop and consistently execute a good system that takes you toward a clear goal, and I will show you how. Just keep reading this book. This book is a breakdown of how I developed a system that took me from a below-average student to a college professor with a doctorate. The *Upgrade Your Life* goal-based system guides you in designing a system to get what you want.

The *Upgrade Your Life* system teaches goal-setting, accountability, emotional intelligence, critical thinking, and discipline so you can take control of your life. It sets you up for success in the game of life. So, what happens when you are in a game you don't know you are in? In the game of Chess, they call that a Pawn. It is a piece that can only be used and is the weakest piece on the board. The game of life separates winners from everyone else. So, how do you play the game of life? You figure out what the winners are doing, and you do that. Then you figure out what people who are not winning are doing, and you don't do that. You are ready to begin your journey when you can accept this basic principle. **Being smart is not a requirement for success.**

In my younger days, I searched for ways to get ahead. I was right where you are. I wanted more out of life. I looked around at the people I went to school with and said there has to be something more to this life. You might notice that many people around you are not getting ahead. But what if you could design the life you want, just like someone would design the house they want to live in? The *Upgrade Your Life* system will help you do just that and more. This system helps you define your goals, create a system, and prepare your mind to reach your goals!

Some of you might be looking for the confidence to start on this new life journey. However, the common myth is that you must have confidence to start. The opposite is usually true. Confidence comes after you have started using the system. However, the more you act on the system you develop in this book, the more confident you become. The Upgrade Your Life system has confidence built into it. Isn't it worth the time to invest in yourself? This book is a significant investment in your future. It is a chance to do something different to reach a different destination in life. If you only do what you have always done, you will only get what you have always got.

People give me so many reasons for not going after their dreams. However, one proven way of achieving your dreams is to build a system that will take you there. It is your magic staircase to wherever you want to go. *Upgrade Your Life* will help you design a system that works. In essence, you will become the answer to your problems. You will become the key that unlocks the door to everything you want in life. And even better than that, this system will prepare you to stay on course until you have reached your goals, that gold at the end of the rainbow.

You are the key to making it all happen, and this book will teach you about becoming the key. Success doesn't just happen. Success is all about becoming the key that opens the doors you want to walk into. Your mind will not allow you to operate in a way inconsistent with your current system. That is why the *Upgrade Your Life* system teaches you the skills to build a system in your mind that will allow you to operate. The system has eight steps:

Upgrade Your Life System

1. Learning systems

2. Analyzing your current system

3. Conditioning your mind for a new system

4. Finding out your strengths and weaknesses

5. Setting and aligning your goals

6. Creating unstoppable motivations for reaching your goals

7. Learning to shift your sight to see success

8. Creating your integrated, goal-based system

Treasure Map to the Gold

Success is not a matter of intelligence. In the 1800s, there was a man who was not considered very smart by the world's standards, but he found a map that led to a fortune in gold. Without hesitation, he followed the map and got the gold. The journey was challenging, but he stayed on course and followed the map. Eventually, he reached his goal, which was gold. He was rich. When he returned to town as a rich man, he was no smarter than anyone else; the only difference was he decided to take action, follow the map, and stay on course. Your success will be determined by how good your map and determination are. The map is the system you build for your life. You do not have to be a genius to get started because you can learn everything you need during your journey.

None of us came into this world knowing everything. We are not born into this world prepared to start a business or become a doctor. We came into this world with great determination. We came into this world determined to eat, sleep, and breathe. You learned everything else along the way. You were not born into this world to read, but if you can read this book, you have successfully learned to read, comprehend, and decide you want a better future. All you need is a good treasure map and a good system for your life.

If you want something bad enough and know how to get it, then it is almost guaranteed that you will get it if you take action. It is not a matter of intelligence. It is a matter of inspiration. All you really need is a system and the right reasons. Don't worry about being the smartest person. Be the person who hires the smartest people. All treasures are locked behind closed doors to protect the wrong people from getting their hands on them. So, you must become the right person if you want the treasure.

The College Myth

What about a college degree? As someone who has spent every year of his life at school since he was four, I can tell you this with certainty: a degree is a tool, not a goal. You can use a degree to get what you want, but avoid using a degree to tell you what you are supposed to be doing. College is not designed to get you a job. College is designed to transform you into someone who can accomplish goals. After teaching in colleges for two decades, I have noticed the hidden challenges facing students entering college and graduating. They have gone through the college system and developed into someone who can succeed; however, the jobs are hard to come by. That is because college is not designed to help you create a system for success. Your responsibility is to set up a system to make yourself into what you want to be so you can have what you want. The *Upgrade Your Life* system is going to help you do just that.

The Unstoppable Key

The unstoppable key is the key that unlocks any door. Behind those doors is everything you want in life, but it takes a special key to unlock these doors. Keys do not start out being able to open doors. They start as a basic-looking key without definition or grooves, so they cannot open doors. They call these keys "blanks" until a key maker cuts them into a shape for a specific lock. Have you ever tried to use the wrong key in a door? That door will never open with the wrong key. All the force in the world will not make that key work. Eventually, the key will break if you use all your strength. For all of you who feel like a broken key, *Upgrade Your Life* has the solution for you.

What you want, you must first become!

What stops many from succeeding? Most people have the wrong idea about where the enemy of success is living rent-free. The thoughts and worries you have brought into your mind are more dangerous than anything scary in the world. The things that destroy you happen from the inside way more than the outside world could ever do. Sometimes, we put up doors and lock ourselves in to be safe while isolating ourselves with the same thoughts that can destroy us. However, I have a word of caution: the same door that keeps out hurt and pain also keeps out joy and happiness. Success is different. Success is often behind closed doors, waiting for the person with the right key to open the door. When you find the doors to your goals shut, you need the right key. The secret is that you are a key ready to be reshaped into the right key, and today is always the right day to start.

Just because you find the door to success locked doesn't mean you are not the key. The key is blank, and you have to develop yourself into the key that unlocks the doors you want to enter. Some doors have a hidden secret; they remain hidden from those who do not possess the knowledge necessary to see the door. Many doors to opportunities will remain invisible to you until you develop into the person to see the door. And the tricky thing about advancing levels is that you see more doors of opportunity you are not designed to open, and you start to get frustrated. You must learn to handle this frustration until you become the key that opens the door. Let me tell you, doors may have been designed to keep people out or to keep something in, but all doors are designed to open. Doors that are not intended to open are called walls. When somebody cannot open the door at all, it means somebody has sealed it shut, and you can move on to the next door.

As long as you live, someone may shut most of the doors of life on you, but most will not be sealed. The right key is the only thing you need to become. How do you know you have the right key? You will see it in the mirror. The final step of this system is becoming the key that will fit any lock. This step is the final key. It is the master key. It is an unstoppable key. *The Upgrade Your Life* system will shape you into the unstoppable key, and you are the key to your better future. You are the unstoppable key!

Sunken Cost Fallacy

Why does developing a system for yourself matter? Well, spending all that time and effort running down a path that doesn't lead you where you want to go would be a tragedy. I encourage you not to waste time on things that move you away from your goals. What happens to all the time you have invested in things that do not move you in the right direction? Should you just let them go? Yes. Count it as the cost of tuition in the School of Life. **If you need the lesson, you pay the tuition.**

Many people suffer from the *sunken cost fallacy*, which occurs when you have spent so much time, money, and energy on something that you feel invested in your decision and do not want to give it up. I knew a guy who sunk so much money into fixing up a car that would never run like he wanted it to. He always said, "I can't quit now, but I have invested too much money into it." Eventually, he sold the car for parts and lost thousands of dollars. He should have learned his lesson earlier, but he wanted to repeat that class, and now he is paying more tuition in the School of Life. I do not want you to have *sunken cost fallacy* with your life. The School of Life is a strange teacher. It likes to give you the test first and the lesson later. You only have this one life to get right. You might as well have a plan. Don't hang on to a mistake because you spent a lot of time making it. Pay less in tuition in the School of Life by learning the lessons from this book. The quicker you learn the lesson, the faster you graduate.

Jim Rohn once said your life does not grow to where you want it to be; it shrinks to where you are. We have to find out where you are. In the *Upgrade Your Life* system, we will find out where you are in life and help you create a great system to take you from where you are to where you want to be. Creating a map leading you anywhere is hard if you do not know where you are starting from. So, what does this mean? You must learn everything about yourself to develop a plan to *Upgrade Your Life*. This self-education will lead to a change in lifestyle and habits to get what you want. There is a price to pay for what you want in life. The trick is to want the right things so that when you pay, you know you got your money's worth. You will get the same result if you keep doing the same old thing. There will be a struggle whether you walk in the right or wrong direction. At least when you design your life using the *Upgrade Your Life* system, you will have a better chance of getting where you want to go.

We don't rise to the level of our goals. We fall to the level of our systems. (James Clear, *Atomic Habits*).

Become system-minded. Most things you buy have a system that delivers them to you the same way every time. Sports teams win based on a system, not individual players' skills. And the best players on that team have systems for how they practice.

What Is Holding You Back?

What is holding you back? Is it fear, laziness, motivation, or not knowing where to start? I have taught thousands of college students and have mentored even more. The biggest thing I have seen that holds people back is fear: fear of failing, getting hurt, wasting time, wasting money, disappointing loved ones, leaving their friends behind, fear of the future, etc.; the list is endless. Fear stops many people from moving forward on the path to success.

Sometimes, the right path with no action will leave you sitting in the same spot. The great hockey player Wayne Gretzky said, "100% of shots never taken are never made." Everything you want involves action. What do you want? How do you find out what you want? Better yet, how do you take action? Well, a good idea without a good system to take you from start to finish will usually only take you so far until the excitement runs out, and then you need a new type of energy to take you the rest of the way to your goals. If you know what you want, this book can show you how to get there without wasting time and relying on excitement to win the race.

Why Are So Many Students Failing?

I talk to many students who are failing and people who are not progressing. One word comes up more than any other the word, and that is the word "fair." They always tell me that people are not being fair to them. Unfortunately, I have to let them know life is not designed around the concept of fairness, and systems are not based on fairness either. Both life and systems are based on goals and outcomes. A system's job is to serve the goals and outcomes it was designed to serve. If you are looking for fairness, you will have better luck walking across the ocean because systems are not based on fairness. The sun comes up in the morning and goes down at night. What if you still need the sunlight to walk home, and the sun goes down? Is that fair? No, it is not. The design of the solar system balances the planets and the sun. The planets revolve around the sun. You may not think that is fair. Maybe you think the planets should be the center of attention sometimes. I do not ask you to like the system, but it would be wise to learn it. Why? Systems are not fair; they are balanced.

Systems assume that whoever is using it has taken the time to understand it, so they know how to operate it. A stove gets hot. It will equally burn good people and bad people. It does not care who touches it. That is the way the system of heat works. That is the **systematic concept of fairness**. When you see someone touch a hot stove and get burned, you hear many people say, "Now, that person has finally learned their lesson." Is it unfair that one person is short and the other is tall? Maybe to some, but *there is a system of biology at work that gathers no opinions from its users.* There is no complaint box. Either you can accept it and learn how to operate within it, or you can be angry and get left behind. If you understand systems, it will reward you. And if you don't understand systems, it will punish you. That is how fairness operates in any system.

Is it unfair that some people pay taxes and others don't? It is unfair from the people's perspective, but the system operates by laws. The ones who don't pay taxes understand the tax system, operate within it and benefit from it. They hire accountants who move their money worldwide and find tax loopholes to keep them from paying taxes. People who don't understand the tax code and system pay more in taxes. The tax system is not based on fairness; it is based on laws. Learn the systems around you, and you will immediately see your life improve. You don't decide your future. Your habits, daily systems, and ability to operate in the systems around you are determining your future right now.

The famous speaker Earl Nightingale once said that America is rigged, not to prevent the strong from winning but to prevent the weak from losing. The entire economy is slowed down to protect the weakest link. We have many systems to keep people from falling too far, but these systems are often designed to create an average outcome. That is why it is so easy to be average; the systems in many countries are designed to produce average results. The *Upgrade Your Life* system will help you build a system that keeps you from being average and takes you to your greatest self.

Are You Really Lazy?

Some people are called lazy, but that may not be the problem. Most people have a goal, so that may not be the problem. Most people I have advised needed a great system to reach their goals. I learned that life is the biggest school, and if you do not figure out the lessons, you must repeat whatever grade level you are in. To pass the grade, you have to come up with your own goals, objectives, lesson plans, and homework. Don't worry about the rest. Life will give you the test and elevate you to the next grade level.

My book will show you a system for developing your personal goals, objectives, lesson plans, and homework that works for each grade level of life. Keep reading, and I will show you what most people do not learn while they are in school. You will have to design a system for passing a class most people do not know they are enrolled in. It is not about being lazy. I know highly motivated, hard-working people who never graduated to the next grade in the school of life. They are smart but have yet to design their life in a way that takes them to the next level. So, they live in someone else's system to survive, which is perfectly fine. Just don't let that be you. Don't lose yourself in someone else's system. Design your system to integrate with other systems in your environment to reach your goals faster. Have you ever been part of a system (team, organization, etc.)? How did your team win? These organizations develop systems for success long before they bring any people in, and every one operates in that system.

Many organizations have two types of employees: worker and creative types. Workers make creative types look lazy. The boss asks workers to mow 100 lawns, and the workers do it immediately. When the boss asks creative types to mow 100 lawns, the creative types sit around waiting for inspiration while looking lazy. The other workers and the bosses get frustrated with creative types. They ask, "Why don't these creative types do as they are told?" Then, the creative types invent the automated lawn mower because they don't want to mow. The creative type makes everyone's job easier with their creativity. They may appear lazy, but many creative people get started differently than workers. I know because I am a creative type.

As Chair of General Studies for a college, I administrated first and second-year general education courses. I worked with so many young people just out of high school. They were trying to accomplish their goals and needed a system to make it happen. I was obsessed with this problem, which led me to create the *Upgrade Your Life* system. I tested the system on several students I was advising, and it turned their lives around. I began using it so much that I incorporated it into my class to reach more people. I helped people build systems to get what they want in life. This book contains my methods for developing a system to achieve what you want. It works! Information is easy to get. Most people need help creating a system of plans and actions. That is what I designed the **Upgrade Your Life** system to do. This system will shift your thoughts and beliefs while reading this book and completing the exercises, and the change process begins in less time than watching a movie.

Is it possible to begin the process of life change in less than the time it takes to watch a movie? And the answer is, "Of course!" Your beliefs and thinking have only brought you this far. Getting to a higher level requires higher thinking. If you don't grow to where you want your life to be, life will shrink to where you are. If you want more, you have to become more. You don't have to be great to get started, but you have to get started to be great. Walk the **Upgrade Your Life** journey and begin the process of being great, and yes, it is a process.

How good are you, and how much better do you need to get? We need to do some assessments to determine your current abilities to accomplish goals. This assessment will deliver a big message, and you will get a different message today than if you read this book a year from now. This book will reveal itself according to where you are in life. I'll prove it to you. Do you think an 8-year-old and a 25-year-old would get the same message from this book? Where are their minds in life? One is thinking about candy and playing with friends, and the other is thinking about a lifetime of experiences. So, the message will be different.

After following the **Upgrade Your Life** system, you will become so motivated because you will have a clear plan to get what you want out of life. This system transforms you into the person you need to be to get what you want. You are going to learn to see more. When you can see more, you will have more options in life. *Upgrade Your Life* is life expansion. This book is going to help you do the following:

- Focus on what you truly want out of life.

- Find out if what you already do is helping or hurting you as you move towards your goals.

- Build an integrated, goal-based system to get what you want out of life.

I am going to guide you through this journey. First, you will be able to learn about systems and what they can do for you. Then, you will closely examine how you are currently running your life. Remember, you are the key that fits the lock to the door you want to enter!

CHAPTER TWO

The Hidden Engine of Success!

Until your system is solid, your goals don't matter. (Lorne Lee)

Have you ever seen people who just succeeded in everything in life? Many of them are not trying to succeed any more than people who are failing are trying to fail; they have a system set up to take them in the direction of success. Trying harder is not the answer. Trying harder for too long is usually a sign your system is not set up correctly. You will never achieve in a way inconsistent with your system.

We all come to this life with an automatic goal-seeking system. It does not understand good or bad. This system takes whatever we focus on the most and builds a path to it. This system assumes the thoughts you are focusing on are your intentional goals. It is like this big machine in our heads activates and then uses our thoughts as GPS coordinates to drive us toward what we focus on the most.

Our job is to take control of this automatic goal-seeking system and use this power to accomplish our goals.

Your system helps you become whatever you are becoming; your goals help you set up your system. You may win a million dollars, but you won't get to keep the money unless you develop a system to become a millionaire in your mind first. It is like someone pouring water into your hands when you are thirsty. You can never hold the water unless you fold your hands in the correct shape to form a cup. You must develop a system to become a person with a millionaire mind to keep a million dollars. We see many people get great things in life, but if you look at their lives over time, you will not know whether or not they have become the person with the skills, knowledge, and character to keep what they have. This book will teach you how to become that person who is the key to what you desire.

How do you become the key that fits the lock to the doors you want to enter? You build a system to turn you (the key blank) into a key that opens doors (the master key). The system you operate shapes you over time. Like watching a key getting made, you can see all of the grooves and edges being cut into the blank key over time. How vital are systems? **Show me your life, and I will show you your systems, and if I can see your systems, I can predict your future.** Looking back over my life, I can see everything I did well had a system built around it.

What Is a System?

A system is a group of interconnected parts that work together to accomplish a specific goal or outcome. These components affect one another, and the system functions within particular limitations.

The most significant limitation is that it only takes you to the goal or outcome according to its design, meaning if you do not like the results, you have to investigate the design. All systems share the common feature of having a goal and using feedback to change and improve itself. Each part of a system is essential in achieving the overall goal. These parts or sections communicate and affect one another in consistent ways, and that consistency leads to a state of balance. The system has ways of gathering information on itself through feedback and data so it can make those changes and improvements. The way the parts of a system are integrated work together is essential for the function and goals of that system.

Assignment: Habit-Based Systems

Our personal systems can go unnoticed most of the day. By a personal system, I mean daily habits. There is a certain way I tie my shoes and brush my teeth every day. These systems are made up of habits. A habit-based system gets things done, so you don't have to think about it. Habit-based actions are the parts of your system that are on autopilot. A habit-based system is good until one day, you realize your life is not working like you want it to. Then, you have to move to a goal-based system. Let's take a moment to check on the habit-based parts of your current system. For this exercise, I want you to write about one area of your life that works well and you don't have to think about, almost like it is on autopilot. Then, write down the habits it takes to get each thing done.

Below, list something that works well.	Below, list at least three habits that get those things done.

All systems work, but most people become angry with the results they get from having a habit-based system without operating a goal-based system at the same time. We need to make sure you are working on goal-oriented systems and monitor your habit-based systems. If you have too many bad habits, your habit-based system will dominate your goal-oriented system until your life stops moving forward. These systems are key to having a better life. It keeps you from being stuck in a dream state. Don't get me wrong; you should have dreams, but dreams without a strategy will always remain an illusion. The difference between who you are and who you want to be is the system you build for yourself now plus time. Know that when you better yourself, you must allow time for everything else to catch up. Time makes the difference.

You exist in a world of systems. Traffic lights, power grids, phones, and social media are all systems. And what about you? Your physical self is a massive combination of integrated systems working together. You have a muscular system, skeletal system, endocrine system, nervous system, respiratory system, digestive system, and cardiovascular system, to name a few. Your heart pumps blood without mental effort, and you can breathe without thought. What about all of the other involuntary systems in your body, like breathing, blinking, and hearing? Your brain has a working system if you can read this or understand what you hear. And all of those systems work together in an integrated system. How powerful is that? We have roads and railway systems that connect across the country. We have ecosystems all over the planets and solar systems all over the universe. Businesses operate using integrated systems. Most of us go through a school system. Since systems govern this whole world, could it be possible to build a system that will take you where you want to go? Yes! Systems are the key to your better future. The more you can understand systems, the better you can build one.

Everything that works well and for any length of time is successful because of a system designed for those results. How can you use the wisdom of systems in your environment to make you constantly successful? First, you must accept one thing: You are already living in other people's systems. So, recognize when you are following someone else's system. As you learn more about systems in this book, you will be able to identify the systems you live in. Look at the systems you are in, name them, and either get on the good side of how things work in that system or get out of them. Learn from the systems all around you.

If you do a little studying, you will notice that every system works according to its design. When life seems to be working against you, the problem usually comes down to three things:

1. A System Designed to Produce Bad Results: A system can produce bad results because all systems work. However, these systems have negative daily actions that will never consistently produce good results. In other words, garbage in, garbage out. The system is a machine that will take whatever you put in it

23

and create something that looks like a combination of every-thing you put in. Check what you are putting in your machine.

2. Do Not Enter Signs: The system may be designed to keep some people out because all systems work. Every system I have seen is designed to safeguard itself to achieve a specific goal.

3. Swimming Against the Current: You do not understand the system, and it seems like the system is working against you because all systems work. However, if you were in a mighty river trying to swim against the current, is the river working against you, or are you going in the wrong direction? If you turn around, swimming is easy. If you do not like where the river is going, get out of the water and find another river.

You will notice there is no option for being unfair. I never said systems were unfair because systems do not operate or understand terms like fair and unfair or right and wrong. They know one thing: They take goal-based actions in their programming and give the only goals those actions can produce. Bad actions produce bad goals. Bad actions can't make good results any more than an apple seed can produce an orange tree. Decide now whether or not you will be in a system that produces good or bad results for you.

There are only two reasons for you to stay in a system producing bad results: 1) if you can help other people by making the system better, or 2) if you have accepted the fate the system has for you. Otherwise, make a plan to leave the system and get out. It might take time to make an exit strategy, but time will go by whether you use it for your benefit or not. You could decide what kind of system you will use because the only thing worse than being in a bad situation for one year is to be in that bad situation for a year and a day without a plan to get out.

What Makes a Goal-Based System Work Well?

A great goal-based system has many characteristics. Here are the elements of a system that produces results well (Gerber, 1995).

- Goals and Objectives: Objectives are specific goals that are measurable and realistically achieved within a certain time frame. In the Upgrade Your Life system, we replace "objectives" with "actions."

- Components: Systems have all the necessary components to work effectively.

- Structure: The system should be organized in a way that makes sense. Each part should connect clearly to other parts, showing how they relate.

- Inputs and Results: The system must quickly handle information that is put into it and generate the results that are needed.

- Feedback Mechanisms. A system needs tools to check its effectiveness, find problems, and make changes when necessary.

- Efficiency and Effectiveness: The system needs to use its resources better and reach its goals.

- Reliability and Durability: The system must be strong enough to handle problems and keep working without stopping.

- Adaptability: The system needs to change and adjust when conditions and requirements change.

- Growth: A good system is designed to grow over time, like a plant is designed to grow continuously.

As you work through this book, decide now that you will only create or participate in a goal-based system.

If all systems work, design one to take you where you want to go. If your system is not working for you, change it to a system that does work. Your system is the secret to giving you the keys to other worlds because you are developing yourself into a key. Some people are born into wealthy worlds where they are free to learn in peace and with all the support they need to be successful. Most people must build systems that transform them into someone who can unlock the doors to success. System builders are not stuck in any world; they connect worlds.

Why do systems win? Because systems build consistency daily, and consistency builds trust. Your system helps you build confidence in yourself. When you have a great system, other people will see the person you are becoming and begin to trust you. That is important because people hire and do business with those they trust. All systems in the universe are successful. However, working harder on a system with the wrong goals is not the magic secret to success; it is the magic path on the road to nowhere. Working hard is important to developing you into the kind of person for which things can work. So, you will need to be more than a hard worker. You need to work hard on the good systems you design. If you want a better life, then get good at building better systems.

People don't decide their future. People determine their habits and actions. Those habits and actions form their system, and their systems shape their future. Systems take you to the future like a rocket ship. The only problem is when the captain doesn't know where the rocketship is going. However, a well-built boat with an average captain, a clear goal, and a good system will always get to its destination, even if it is the slowest ship in the world.

Successful and unsuccessful people usually have the same goals but drastically different systems. In addition, the successful person commits to the system. The people who are not successful usually commit to the goals and ignore the system. They end up committing to wishful thinking. You must have goals to get started, but you must have a good system built on those goals to reach your destinations.

We are all operating in a world of systems. The question is: Do you like the results your system gives you? How do you become the person you want to be and have the things you want to have while using your current system? Also, if your system is working, could you improve it to get you more? I once heard of a guy who built a business making chicken sandwiches. He figured if he sold 100 sandwiches a day at $5 a sandwich, he could make $500 a day and have a good life He worked all day to make 100 sandwiches. By the end of the day, there was no more time to make more sandwiches, and he was so tired after working seven days a week that he had no time for his family. On top of all that, his system maxed out at $500 a day.

This guy's system was working but not moving him towards his goals. His real goal was to spend time with his family, and he couldn't do that by making and selling 100 chicken sandwiches a day. So, he decided to franchise his business. He sold the rights to use his chicken sandwich system to 1,000 people for $500 a day each in franchise fees. Now, he makes $500,000 a day without making a single chicken sandwich, and he spends every evening and all weekend with his family. That is the power of a good chicken sandwich backed by a good system. Would he have ever accomplished his goals if he kept making 100 sandwiches daily and had not improved his system? No. Like the previous example, ask yourself if you could improve your system to reach your goal. And the answer is absolutely yes!

Integrated Systems

An integrated system is made up of different parts called subsystems. These subsystems work together smoothly to reach a shared goal. Imagine it like a puzzle, where every piece connects perfectly to form a complete picture. If you've ever flown on an airplane, you have experienced an integrated system. Yes, the planes are designed to fly with the systems built into the plane, but there is a vast network of air travel routes that constantly cross each other, like busy traffic at an intersection. Without a system in place, the planes run into each other. All airline routes are monitored by aircraft controllers with local systems integrated into a vast national and international system that directs the traffic in the sky. This is a massive integrated system. The next step to your success is understanding how your system integrates with other successful systems to get you where you want to go, just as the plane got where it needed to go by combining with other successful systems.

How many systems are in your body? All those systems working together is an example of an integrated system. Each system works in harmony with the other systems in your body to support your life. As you make systems for your life, think of them as one integrated system working towards a common goal. All these separate subsystems work together to develop you into the person who will be the key to your success.

So, how are these systems built? You build these systems using intentional actions and daily habits. Habits are actions you do not have to think about. You want intentional habits that support your goals. You want to be in control of your habits. If not, your habits will soon control you. The more consistent and intentional your daily habits and actions are, the more consistent your life will be. The more intentional you are about those habits and actions, the more you will get what you intend to get out of life. The *Upgrade Your Life* system will challenge you to see if you are truly committed because, throughout your life, you will face the ultimate hurdle: inconsistency.

Inconsistency ruins business, marriages, and anything else it touches. What happens to flowers that don't get watered regularly? Even worse, what happens to children whose parents do not spend consistent time with them? Inconsistency ruins everything it touches. Rule # 1 is to be consistent. Build your system for consistency, not speed. The journey is challenging, but the rewards are big! So, don't join an easy crowd by putting this book down. Be consistent and read your way to success. Create a system for how many pages of *Upgrade Your Life* you read daily.

Get on the good side of the way things work. You don't have to like how things work; you just have to accept it and get on the good side or get out. The sun goes down at the same time every night, depending on the season. What if a doctor was in the forest operating to save someone's life and needed the sun for light just as the sun was going down? That's not fair. I don't ask you to like it. It is just how things work, and we accept it. Nobody goes around yelling at the sun for going down. So, get on the good side of how things work. Get on the good side of the systems in your life. Create a system around the existing systems in your environment, and you will learn how to be successful.

Let's look at your current system and see if it gives you the life you want. Is your current system designed to shape you into the key to the doors of your goals? Remember, you are the leader of your life and the key to your success. You are the key that fits the lock to the door you want to enter!

CHAPTER THREE

Are Your Habits Killing You or Rewarding You?

In this chapter, you will learn how well your current system works. We all have been shaped into the person we are, but it is up to us to shape ourselves into the person we want to become. It is your responsibility to shape yourself, or your environment will forever shape you. You have already been shaped into a key that fits particular doors. What doors would you be able to open? If you are unsure, let me ask a question to help clarify things. What doors can you open for others? When you know the answer to that question, you know what kind of key you are. You will know what kind of key you are when you see how you can help others.

For years, I only helped people in music. Then, one day, I stopped teaching music and started teaching people to reach their goals. I changed and became a new key. Suddenly, I could open new doors and access new opportunities that seemed impossible. Everything came so quickly because I was not trying to break into a door I had no key for. I based my new system on helping people, and that new system developed me into a new person. I became the key to a new door of opportunities.

Right Door...Wrong Key!

What doors do your current keys open? Some people keep getting bad results because their keys only open the wrong doors. We need to see what kind of keys you have. Your key does not work on broken locks, so it opens doors for you; the question is, which one? Your key will not work in a door it was not designed to open, but keys open all doors, good and bad. So, if your key keeps opening the wrong doors, that should be a clue that you need to change into a key that will open the right doors, which leads me to our next rule: **Stay away from wrong doors! You might accidentally find out your key fits!**

Keys have no sense of right and wrong; they just open doors. Opening any door makes a key successful, but that has nothing to do with what is behind the door. What doors do your current keys open? Have you developed yourself into the key to the right doors? Do you know how to find the right doors? Understanding the importance of keys is the first step in the *Upgrade Your Life* system.

It is time to learn more about yourself and where you are in life. As I said in Chapter 1, creating a system leading you anywhere is hard if you do not know where you are starting from. My father used to say, "Who you are is a fact. What you are becoming is the truth." It took me a long time to get this lesson, but he was saying that what you see when you look in the mirror is real, but it may not be true. Yes, you may be someone who did not do well in school. You may not be doing well in life. That is real. But that is not the truth of who you are. It may be the system you have been operating with up until now. It may be time for a systems upgrade.

Over the years, I have taught and advised thousands of college students and discovered some common traits of people who take longer to get ahead in life. They all have reasons for not doing well. Some people may call them reasons, but I call them excuses. The biggest problem is when people mistake excuses for reasons. Do you have a list of excuses for not doing well? Do you ever call any of those excuses "reasons"?

Doing life as you have always done may not be the path to success. If doing what you've always done would work, it would already be working. So, life will only change when you decide to change. Change a little if you want things to change a little. Change a lot if you want things to change a lot. Just choose to change. Make a decision that you are going to change. A decision is different than a choice. A choice is saying there are other options to choose from. A decision says there are other options, but this is the option I am committed to, and I will not turn back. One person says they will eat pizza today and then a salad tomorrow. Whatever they choose will be fine. That is a choice. The other person says I am tired of being unhealthy and will not eat junk food anymore! Now, that is a decision. **Decisions have power built into them**.

Everything you are looking for is on the other side of the person you need to become. Don't look for your goals in your current system. All you will find is what you already have. Your life is like water. It will flow towards whatever path you have dug for it. Life always takes the path of least resistance unless it is diverted for a purpose, which makes digging a system a little more complicated. You must design your life to flow toward your goals before the floods of life leave you stranded at sea. If you have not dug a path to a new location, just expect your life to go with the flow, which, for many, is down the drain.

If you live in this world, you live surrounded by thousands of systems. The best way to win in a systematic world is to have the best systems for yourself. I will help you build one as you read and complete this book. Even if you do not like reading books, I encourage you to complete this book. Develop a system for finishing this book. The system could be, "I read 5 pages of the *Upgrade Your Life* system daily." Make your statement action words in the present tense, then do it. Magically, you will have completed the book in a month, drastically changing your life. People will say it is magic because a really good system will look like magic to the world when completed. Who do you want to be? We are about to build a goal-oriented system for whoever you want to be. That is exciting!

You are about to be better by design. If you want something, you don't wish for it; you design a way to get it. Design a system. Ask any sports team that has won a championship. They did not wish for that championship. The coach developed a practice schedule and a daily system that worked. The goal those coaches have in mind is for the students to take the principles of the system to win championships and use those systems to win in the game of life.

Life in the Magic Jar

Life is like putting money in a jar. You can never fit more than the size of the jar. The problem is that some people's jars are so small inside that they can only hold a few pennies. That is called small thinking. And others seem to be in debt. That is called wishful thinking. But others figured out this thing called life, and they started becoming more. That is called smart thinking. Life wants to pour into you, but it cannot pour into three things: a jar that is too small, a jar with a closed lid, and a full jar. A full jar must be poured out or grow bigger to receive more. So, think of life as something happening from inside of you and not something happening to you from out there. You are the magic jar. If you become bigger on the inside, the life inside you will grow to fill up all of the new extra space. If you grow, your life can grow because you are the key to upgrading your life.

The Gardener

You can get what you want, but your life may be too small to keep it until you grow to become the person your goals are built for. Interestingly enough, if you become that person, you can lose everything you have and still get it back again. The universal law says that life comes back to where you are. If you cut down a tree, it will just grow right back. If you cut grass, it will grow back. Everything in this world grows to its capacity. A puppy successfully grows into a dog every time. Nature will not trick us by growing the dog into a cat. It will be a dog every time. And the garden of your life will grow whatever you plant there. If you plant corn, you can't expect lettuce to grow. You can plant corn in million-dollar soil and water it every day, but the only plant you will get is corn. Life is the same way. So, lesson number one is that you get what you plant. If you don't like the crops, the first person to question is the planter, and you can find that person in the mirror. So, plant well and tend to your garden at all times. It is all you got. Without a garden, your success will surely starve. So, how do you build a garden? You plan it and develop a system to grow the crops you want. Then, you protect your garden until harvest time.

Just like planting a garden, the farmer has to plant the seed, knowing that the seed will be deep in the dirt and out of the spotlight for a long time. No one will see the planting, but everyone will stop to admire the crops. The farmer must work with the intention to grow in the garden. On top of that, the farmer will not know when the rain is coming. And patience is necessary for this garden. The day you plant the seed is not the day you eat the fruit. Be patient and rememer you are you are working towards a bountiful harvest. That is the nature of the garden of where you are growing in your life. You do not know when the big payoff is going to be. You just know that it will come in due season.

Make It a Study

Whatever you want out of life, make it a study. And then make it a goal-based system. Don't leave it to chance. Make it a system. For people in school, you work 8 hours a day on someone else's system designed to improve yourself. What happens after you leave school? After finishing school, you have to make a system to improve yourself. Nobody is going to teach you how to make this system. That is your responsibility. And besides, it is too complicated because each system is as unique as your fingerprint. Another person's fingerprint system will not give access to the doors of your goals. So, make everything a study. Jim Rohn used to say, "You may not be able to do all you can find out, but you should find out all you can do." And while studying, take some

3: ARE YOUR HABITS KILLING YOU OR REWARDING YOU?

time to study history, especially the history of whatever you want in life. Studying history is like reading tomorrow's newspaper today because what goes around comes around. There is nothing new under the sun. Do you want proof? Would you lend money to someone who wastes it? No. That is because you know their history. Study the history, requirements, and current trends of whatever you want in life.

The Perfect Person to Study

One of the best ways to get ahead is to study and learn from other people's mistakes, but a great way to learn is to examine your mistakes. Learn from your past. It is a great teacher because it is the best way to learn about yourself and why you are the way you are now. Look at the results of your life now, and if you don't like them, look at your past and find out what went wrong. Once you know that, you will know more about how to fix problems in your life.

Why Do So Many Businesses Fail Within the First Five Years?

Even if you have a system, your system has to be designed to achieve specific goals. Since this is supposed to be common knowledge in business, why do most fail? According to the Bureau of Labor Statistics (U.S. Bureau of Labor Statistics, (2024), approximately 20% of small businesses fail in their first year. The failure rate increases to 30% by the end of the second year, 50% by the fifth year, and 70% by the tenth year. 80% fail by year 20. I don't know about you, but I plan to live more than 20 years. Wouldn't it be good to understand why they fail so you do not have to? Let's take a look at why businesses with systems still fail.

Here are four big reasons businesses fail: they do not plan well; they do not carry out their plans with good management; businesses do not understand the needs of their market (the customers) by doing the research; and they underestimate the cost of doing business (Mayr et al., 2021). So, how can you learn from each of these reasons? Let's say you were building a huge building. What would happen if the four reasons for business failure were excuses used by the construction company building the skyscraper with 100 floors? Would you want to ride to the top of a building in an elevator installed by a company with bad plans, poor management, uninformed leaders, and not knowing how much money to bring to finish building the building? Do you think they may have added all of the expensive safety cables for the elevator, or would they have chosen the cheaper cables of less quality? Companies do this all the time. They cut corners to cut costs. You can cut corners when baking cookies but not when installing an elevator. By the time the elevators break, the elevator company is long gone.

Don't let what you build in your life collapse because of the big four reasons for business failure. But you are not going to let that happen. You will create your system the right way and manage it well. You will count the cost before you start and understand the people in the world you want to go into. Only high achievers have a system for life like the one you are building in *Upgrade Your Life*. Success is built and sustained by planning a system to get there and stay there, so welcome to the group of high achievers.

Systems That Work: Lessons from Great Systems

Let's look at examples of excellent systems. These systems are not usually exciting; they are effective. They work! The excitement comes from your reasons and goals. Don't look for excitement in the system; look for effectiveness. Here are three great systems you should know about. McDonalds, Amazon, & Apple all have much better systems than their competitors. McDonald's delivers consistency throughout its nearly 42,000 restaurants in the world. Their burgers are not the best, but their systems are second to none. Their identity is the basis for their system; they sell affordable food fast in a fun and dependable way. They are customer-focused. Their system is so good that they never run out of food

(Dittfurth et al, 2024). Another great system is Amazon. Amazon delivers with unmatched consistency. They have a system that has changed the way people shop. They are innovative and customer-focused (Aversa et al., 2021; Hassel & Sieker, 2022). The last is Apple, Inc., which has created a system of brand loyalty so effective that its customers never leave. They have a system of loyalty, trust, and innovation so impressive that customers know governments can't hack or access their phones (Steinwart & Ziegler, 2014). They are innovative, consistent, and are customer-focused.

There are three main qualities that we can learn from studying these companies. They focus on how they can serve others. These companies are always looking for ways to solve more people's problems through innovation and are very consistent at all levels of their business. To win in this game of life, study the success secrets of these companies by focusing on the needs of the people you want to do business with, anticipating future needs through innovation, and mastering the art of delivering on your promise 100% of the time.

Discipline is a master key to success. Discipline involves consistency in carrying out your system. The best sports legends say discipline beats natural talent and ability every time. Think about someone significant in a sport. They train and practice thousands of hours only to show 3 hours of that skill in a game. People will never see most of the hard work you put into developing and carrying out the system that took you to your goals. However, your system's actions and daily habits are the price you pay for what you want. Now that you understand what makes a good system, let's check your system's alignment.

Alignment

How well does your life align? In this section, we will see if your actions align with your goals and if your goals align with your beliefs. Why is alignment so important? All systems have alignment. Your bones have to be in alignment for them to function. An army has to be in alignment by following a chain of command to win wars. Your car has to be in alignment for it to drive straight. Maintaining alignment is very important as you go after your goals. What would happen if you drove down a straight road and got out of alignment with the road just slightly? Within minutes, you will end up in a ditch on the side of the road or headed into oncoming traffic; either way, it is dangerous for you and everyone around you.

The destructive nature of the unfocused mind shows up in your life even more because life is not a straight road. It has all kinds of twists and turns, so make a promise to yourself right now to keep your eyes on the road and your hands on the steering wheel for the rest of your life. It is better to accept it than to fight this one; you might as well fight a storm from dropping rain. Alignment is critical to any system, and focus is needed to stay aligned.

Assignment: Systems Check

This section will help you determine what system level you are operating on. We act like we are the victims of how things are, but in reality, we are the victims of who we are and the operating system we use. Why do we deal with systems in this book? The biggest reasons businesses fail and cars break down on the side of the road are system failures. So, we have to check your systems to make sure you are not about to break down on your way to your goals. Your system level indicates how well your system is taking you toward the current goals you will design in the goal-setting chapter of this book. The aim is to see how well your systems align with your goal. If your goals need to be in better alignment, that is okay. Your goals will align if you learn all the lessons and complete all the activities in this book. It is time to evaluate how effective your current system is. For this exercise, write habits or actions you don't have to consider, almost like they are on autopilot. That is your system. Give each action and habit a number. This number is the level at which you believe the action or habit is taking you toward your goal. Next, write down all the ways your system is taking you towards your goals in life. Follow the steps below.

Step 1: Write your daily actions or habits. These are habits other than eating and daily hygiene. Write your answer in the chart after the example. Use another document to write down your answers if you needed.

Step 2: Give each action or habit a goal number from 0 to 10. A score of 0 is the lowest and means the action or habit is taking you directly away from your goals. A score of 10 is the highest and means the action or habit is taking you directly to your goal. A score in the middle is not helping or hurting. Middle scores (like a 5) on your list may help you get through the day but may not help you achieve your goals. Many actions and habits that keep you relaxed also keep you in the same place in life. Your job is to find out what these actions and habits are so you can find out why you are getting the results you are getting. This section is critical for advancing your life.

- A score of 9-10 means the action or habit directly supports your goals.

- Actions and habits that partially support your goals score between 6-8.

- Actions and habits that do not support your goal but do not work against your goals get a score of 4-6.

- Actions and habits that indirectly work against your goals (such as playing video games, watching social media, etc.) get a score of 1-3.

- Actions and habits that destroy your goals (such as engaging in any form of criminal activity, fighting, drugs, alcohol, etc.) earn a score of 0.

Write your answer in the chart after the example.

Step 3: Write how much time you spend on each habit daily.

Step 4: Totals

- Write the total number of habits and multiply it by ten. **___ Habits x 10** = ___

- Add up your total score. **Score ___**

- Divide your total score by the number of habits. **___ divided by ___** = ___

- Move the decimal over two places to get your percentage: **___ becomes ___%**

- Add up your total time. **___ hours**

- Your system spends **___ hours a day** operating at ___%.

Example:

Action or Habit	Score	Time Spent
Watching funny videos on social media	3	2 hours a day
Reading books about your chosen career path	9	1 hour a day
Going to the gym	5	1 hour a day

- Write down the total number of habits and multiply it by ten. **3 Habits x 10 = 30**

- Add up your total score. **Score 17**

- Divide your total score by the number of habits. **17 divided by 30 = .56**

- Move the decimal over two places to get your percentage: **.56 becomes 56%**

- Add up your total time. **4 hours a day**

- Your system spends **4 hours a day** operating at **56%**.

A score of 56% lets you know your system is failing to move you toward your goals. You're not failing; your system is failing. Now that you know your system is failing, you can improve it or create a new one.

Steps 1-3: Write your actions or habits in the first, score them in the second column, and write your time in the third column.

Action or Habit	Score	Time Spent

- Write the total number of habits and multiply it by ten. **___ Habits x 10 = ___**

- Add up your total score. **Score ___**

- Divide your total score by the number of habits. **___ divided by ___ = ___**

- Move the decimal over two places to get your percentage: **___ becomes ___%**

- Add up your total time. ___ **hours**

- Your system spends ___ **hours a day** operating at ___%.

You have just completed your first daily actions and habits analysis of yourself. Most people never make it this far in life. They just think about it casually, but you are being intentional. Congratulations!

Assignment: Identity Statement

Who do you believe you are? Now is the time to make a statement about who you are. This statement can change anytime, but now you must decide whether to be like everyone else or upgrade your life. Write a one-sentence statement telling the world who you are and your life mission.

```
┌─────────────────────────────────────────────────────┐
│                                                     │
│                 Identity Statement                  │
│                                                     │
│                                                     │
│                                                     │
│                                                     │
└─────────────────────────────────────────────────────┘
```

You are already the ultimate system, but you did not design yourself. Over the years, you began to create systems for yourself. You made your system so good that it doesn't matter if you change your mind about what you want to do. Your system still works as designed. Let's take a closer look. You were a baby, and now you have grown into an adult. That is a system that works. It works almost on autopilot. Are there other systems that work on autopilot in your life? What about all of the other involuntary systems in your body, like breathing, blinking, and blood circulation? All of us even have a nervous system in our bodies. If you can read this sentence, your brain has a system that is working at an advanced level. You are already living in the ultimate system, and when the system is functioning, the results are automatic. It's all about having an automatic system based on the goals you want.

Assignment: Inventory Part 2 - Know Thyself

The most important person to study is yourself. Understanding yourself is so important. How do you think, and how do you learn?

1. How do you learn? Knowing how you learn can make you a better student in the school of life than you could ever imagine. It does not matter how old you are. If you know how you learn, you can grow your knowledge faster. Let's find out about your learning style. Most people have more than one style. Are you more of a (Circle all that apply):

   b. Visual Learner: I learn by watching others.

   c. Auditory Learner: I learn by listening.

   d. Visualizer Learner: I visualize myself doing the task in my head.

   e. Active Learner (Hands-on): I learn by doing.

   f. Textual Learner: I learn by reading.

2. Are you a leader or a follower? _____

3. Are you proactive or reactive? _____

4. How do you handle a crisis? (circle your answer)

   e. Take action

   f. Stop everything and think

g. Wait for help

h. Procrastinate

i. Run and hide

5. What are you good at (your strengths and skills)?

6. What are your weaknesses?

7. How can you improve the top three things you are bad at? (Write this down on a separate sheet of paper.)

8. How can you improve on your weaknesses? (Write this down on a separate sheet of paper.)

What are the top five things that are important to you? Include the important areas of your life. (Write this down on a separate sheet of paper.)

On a scale of 1-10 (10 being the highest), how good are you at finishing what you start? _____

On a scale of 1-10 (10 being the highest), how much can people depend on you? _____

On a scale of 1-10 (10 being the highest), how much can you depend on yourself? _____

This next set of questions is based on the Big Five Personality Traits, also known as OCEAN or CANOE, are a psychological model that describes five broad dimensions of personality types: Openness, Conscientiousness, Extraversion, Agreeableness, and Neuroticism (O'Connor & Paunonen, 2007).

On a scale of 1-10 (10 being the highest), how curious and open-minded are you (Openness)? _____

On a scale of 1-10 (10 being the highest), how organized and disciplined are you (Conscientiousness)? _____

On a scale of 1-10 (10 being the highest), how outgoing and sociable are you (Extraversion)? _____

On a scale of 1-10 (10 being the highest), how cooperative and trusting are you (Agreeableness)? _____

On a scale of 1-10 (10 being the highest), how emotionally stable are you (Neuroticism)? _____

You do not need to judge the list, but you need to know yourself. If areas on the list need improvement, then start improving them. However, when you finish the Upgrade Your Life system, you will learn how to build a system to fix your issues.

Other Questions to Ask Yourself

Are you emotionally fit to handle failures? Are you emotionally fit to handle success? How you handle failures is usually how you handle success. People who make loud outbursts for failures also make loud outbursts for success. How do you handle failures? What is your bounce-back time? Everyone gets knocked down, but life is about your recovery time and how quickly you can recover.

Keep this in mind: You are the leader of your life! Winning and losing in life starts from the inside out. If you want your life to change, start changing from the inside. Don't look for someone to come and save you. You could be waiting longer than you think. It is time to Upgrade your Life and save yourself. The future YOU is coming to save your life. The better you make your Upgrade Your Life system, the quicker it will happen. You are the key to the door of your goals! And know that you know yourself better, let's jump inside the mind of a champion.

CHAPTER FOUR

Mindset: Get the Mind of a Champion

What you want, you must first become!

Get ready to make a significant leap in your life. Before we build your goal-based system, you have to condition your mind to become the key to your success and survival. The journey is not easy, so you need a survival kit for your mind. Your mind may resist the new system because the old system will be fighting for survival, and your mind may attach itself to that old system. So, this is where we condition you to take power over your mind and take on the mind of a champion.

Conditioning the mind comes before all the other steps. If you miss this part, the other *Upgrade Your Life* system steps may not work for you. If you change your circumstances before changing your mindset (the way you think), those circumstances will soon fall back to the condition of the mind. However, if you memorize these lessons, you could save 20 years of frustration and disappointment. You could avoid the struggle you see other people go through if you make the mindset lessons in this chapter a part of your thinking.

Be Like the Bamboo Tree

Bamboo is one of the fastest-growing trees on Earth and one of the slowest-developing plants on the planet. The bamboo tree takes 3 to 5 years to develop its roots underground, but after five years, something magical happens. After five years of work being done underground, the bamboo tree grows 90 ft in just five weeks and can grow 18 inches in 24 hours (Chen et al., 2022). The bamboo tree has to be watered and fertilized, even as it is underground and can't be seen. The gardener is watering and taking care of something important, while people who are unaware judge the gardener for this waste of time. But the gardener knows the value of what will happen in 3-5 years.

This is how your life will be. You will work underground in the shadows, getting no credit. Then, you will have your breakthrough. One day, people will see you rise like a bamboo tree and say you are an overnight success, but they don't know it was a ten-year night. The years you worked that other people could not see made everything possible. Be patient and follow the system you are building in this book. All success is measured over time. So, expect your success to happen in the same way. If you want to know how well you are doing, measure your life over time because your systems will take you on a journey to your goal of success over time. You may not know, but you have already started the system-building process. The obvious parts come later in this book. However, the part that will make your life like the bamboo tree is developing right now through the words you are reading.

Winning the Inner Fight: Ready vs. Prepared

Being ready is a mindset. You may be ready to go on a trip, but are you fully prepared? Have you packed everything you need and made all your plans to be ready for your destination? Some people are prepared but never get ready. But if they knew how prepared they were, all they need to do is take their leap.

Changing your mindset with the *Upgrade Your Life* system may feel more challenging at first. It's like working out. When you start, you don't get stronger; you get weaker first. Your muscles hurt. Then, over time, it becomes easier. And with the shift you are about to undertake, you may experience weakness. You are developing a strength that doesn't come easy. I will not trick you by saying changing your life is easy. That is why most people don't do it. It may not be easy, but I promise you, it will be worth it.

There will also be a fight for survival. The old you will fight every thing you do to become better or worse because the old you is fighting for survival. The *old you* can not come where the *current you* is going, and without the current you, the *old you* will fade into history. So expect every trick in the book from the old you. You can win this inner fight as long as you know you are in a fight. When you are in a fight, your guard is up, and you expect the punches. You can brace for them and learn how to defend yourself. If you do not know how to fight, you quickly learn how to fight for yourself. You are the only one who can fight the inner fight for your life. A critical step in the *Upgrade Your Life* system teaches us that what you say when you talk to yourself is very important. There is a battlefield of language. The words you say to yourself will give you the winning edge in this inner fight. Winning the inner fight is the first step to winning the race in life.

Get serious about finishing well. Don't let everyday life distract you from your purpose and goals. You can't run a race loaded down with distractions. Look at a track team. They may work out with heavy weights, but they win the race by developing strength with weights and running without the same weights that would slow them down. The weight that weighs them down is only designed to make them strong and never to carry in the race. To run this race of life, you have to unload the attitudes, thoughts, and emotions that can slow you down. If you are alive, you are in the race. So how do you win? If you carry those heavy mental weights around on your daily walk, your walk may slow down to a crawl. If you want to go faster, find out what is weighing you down emotionally and unload it. And what do you do with distractions? LOOK AWAY. Lock your eyes on your goals while concentrating on the system you build for yourself in this book.

Your success is more about how you think and what is taking most of your attention than what you know. Whatever you are looking for, you will eventually find. It is all about your eyes. If you look for the bad in a situation or the good, you will find it because both are there. So it is your choice. What do you want to look for? You can guard yourself against danger without searching for it, or you can take on the mind of danger and find it everywhere because whatever you are looking for, you will find it. Our minds are designed for survival. It is programmed to find anything we spend our time thinking about. Your mind is also designed to ignore what you are not thinking about all day. Your mind must take in so much information that it needs to ignore some information to use its power to see what you think about the most.

When you think about your goals and daily actions associated with those goals, your mind will point out everything that can help you achieve those goals. So, prepare for danger, but spend all your time thinking about your goal-based systems. You may not know it, but with every page you are reading, you are in the mental conditioning stage of the *Upgrade Your Life* system. By reading these words, you are preparing your mind for the challenge of building a goal-based system that will give your life a power you have never known.

What You Want, You Must First Become!

What does that mean? This means that if someone gives you control of an airplane, you better become a pilot before taking control of the plane, or the flight will not go as planned. The quickest way to crash your life is to get something you are not ready for. It is like handing a child keys to the car; all you will do is set the child up for disaster. The same principle applies to many arenas of life. Some lottery winners lose all their money this way. They get millions without becoming and developing the mindset of a millionaire, so they eventually lose the money. That is because life will always shrink down to where you are. A million dollars will eventually shrink down to the $30,000 mind it has been given to. The person will spend the million dollars on cars and vacations until all they have left is $30,000.

How many times have you seen professional athletes make millions only to end up broke after the paychecks stop coming? It happens all the time. If you do not become what you are trying to have, life will shrink to where you are and hold you captive by your limitations. But if you possess a millionaire mind and I give you $30,000, your money will soon go to a million dollars! First, become it and then possess it.

What you want, you must first become. Act like the person who has what you want, even when you are not there yet. These days, everything is being recorded for future use, and whatever you say now can and will be used for you or against you. You don't want to become the CEO of a major company just to have your image torn down by who you used to be because old pictures and videos of you are viewed online worldwide. If you want a professional image later, the work starts now. You will not always be where you are. You will not always be a student or whatever you are doing now. Become who you want to be and act accordingly now.

Imagine you received a $10 million contract to play football without being a good football player or even being in good shape. Would you be ready? Would you be able to keep your job after the first game? What about the first practice when the coaches and teammates noticed you were not a professional-level football player? People can look at you and tell you are not shaped like an NFL player. After the first practice, you might even get hurt. To get the $10 million to play professional football, you must first become a professional-level football player. It takes years of training and dedication to get to that level. Unless you become what you seek, you will never get to keep it. And if you won the lottery for a million dollars, you had better become a millionaire quickly so you can keep the money. Otherwise, you will see it go faster than water going down the drain. **Rule of Life: If you do not grow out to where life is, life will shrink to where you are**.

What about confidence? You don't have to be ready to start. No one begins something they don't think they can finish. Most of the time, we see ourselves mentally completing something before we start. We imagine and fantasize about it. Can you count on yourself? When you know you can, your life will leap forward from imagination to reality. You can win if you develop and consistently execute a goal-based system. You do not have to be smart to start. You don't even need confidence to start. Just get a good system and work it. Don't worry. The system you build in this book will give you confidence automatically by design.

To carry out the system, you must become best friends with patience. Some people look at successful people and say wow, they were an overnight success. They may say that, but they may not realize that it was a ten-year night. The night lasts long, even for an overnight success, so patience has to become your best friend. Growth happens like a tree. You may not see the growth, but you will notice that the tree has grown over time. The fruits may sprout quickly, but don't mistake the fruit for growth.

After patience is passion; passion is love on fire. It is love for a goal, family, or anything you desire. It burns like a flame that will not go out, and that is the passion you need. Passion can be a success advantage. Be passionate about your goals and fascinated about life; both will open up to you. If you love life, it will love you right back.

Be passionate about knowledge. The value you place on the knowledge you are receiving will determine how well you can focus. I will prove it. If I said that you have to sit in a chair for 10 minutes to learn the plans of how to get a million dollars that was hidden in a secret location, how easy would it be to sit and focus for 10 minutes? You wouldn't be thinking about anything else. The intense feeling of wanting a million dollars tells you it is worth sitting there focusing. Nothing else matters at that point because the value is too high. But if I asked the average person to listen for 10 minutes, and I would tell you the secret location of a book with the secrets of the millionaire's mind, would they even pay attention? If they don't, then they do not put a value on knowledge. That is where you can have the advantage. Be fascinated with knowledge, and you will be ahead of many. Be fascinated with the knowledge that will take you towards your goals, and you will be ahead of most people.

Believe in Yourself

Doubt creates more failures than bad luck ever will. (Lorne Lee)

If you do not believe, you will produce doubt, and failure will become a self-fulfilling prophecy. You will think you are a failure because doubt creates more failures than bad luck ever will. To turn it all around, you must believe in your system for achieving success. It's about what you say when you talk to yourself. Then your actions will become more confident. You can never go beyond your ideas about yourself.

Believing in yourself is directly related to discipline. If a person doesn't have the discipline to follow through on their promises to themselves, they begin a process that is hard to reverse. Some people do not believe in themselves because they have broken promises to themselves so often that they don't think a word they say. People don't see you through their eyes. They see you through your eyes and how you see yourself. If you do not have confidence in yourself, don't expect anyone else to either.

And don't stay in environments where people refuse to recognize your value. If you do, you will shrink your gifts to the size of what other people can handle. In every hero's journey throughout history, the hero had to leave their environment to have the transformation (Campbell, 2014). Sometimes, you have to leave your environment to become more than you are. It affects your beliefs about yourself; whatever you believe about yourself, you will rise or lower yourself to that truth. The *Upgrade Your Life* system will guide you in developing all the confidence you need to start and the discipline you need to finish, which will become the key to your success.

Attitude

Your attitude will help determine how quickly and well you become the key to success. The attitude of gratitude is a success principle. Having an attitude of gratitude makes everyone want to help you even more. Gratitude gives you optimism, and like Dr. Joshua Oyekan used to say, optimism is the lubricant that keeps the wheels moving. Being optimistic can be difficult when things go wrong, but one of the requirements for this journey is to keep your thinking more positive than negative. Negative people get stuck in the quicksand of their own emotions. If you are negative in your thinking or don't have enough passion for your purpose, any excuse will work to stop you from going for your goals.

Keeping positive can free you up to move forward because where focus goes, energy flows. When I focus on my goals, I am optimistic. Then, my mind focuses on things that will move me in a positive direction. I can reflect on my time journal, which will tell me so. The thing I get excited about the most is my ability to make myself do what needs to be done without complaint. The power you have to take action in your life is exciting!

Decision Making: The Hardest Part

Being decision-minded can take you further than being smart. Life passes most people by while they are making grand plans for it. The hardest part about making plans is deciding to get started. There is a difference between making a choice and making a decision. Making a choice is about picking between options. Making a decision is about crossing a bridge and cutting the ropes to that old wooden bridge so you can never return. It is cutting off all other options. And indecision is a bad decision. You do not have to be ready. You just have to be prepared. You better prepare for your future because you will spend the rest of your life there. Make a decision, prepare yourself, and go after it. Life gives you everything else you need to know after you get started, not in the preparation phase.

Don't let fear of what other people say stop you. Aristotle said, "To avoid criticism, do nothing, say nothing, and be nothing." I promise that if you hide in a corner, people will soon forget about you. But when you go for your goals, people will criticize you. It is part of the journey. However, when you are really in the race for your goals, crowds of people will be standing on the sidelines of life, waiting to see if you will finish this marathon. It is a race against yourself, so no one will care who reaches the finish line first.

Getting Started

You don't have to be ready to start something. You need to make sure you have prepared as much as possible and know that you will get the rest along the way. Your level of preparation is what makes you ready. Your belief in yourself is what makes you stay.

Don't wait for the feeling. Just start being what you want to become because everything finds itself. Knowledge finds the wise person. Love finds a heart full of love, and success finds the person who has developed into a successful person. That is the first step on your journey. You can't get ready enough for the opportunities coming. It's like being at the swimming pool when the water is cold; you must jump in at some point.

So many people wait for the perfect time to start. Perfection excuses are self-sabotage on the road to success. Having to make sure everything is perfect before you start turns into an excuse because we all know there is no such thing as human perfection. Perfection is a trap and self-sabotage. However, if you get started, you will find perfection in finishing. Don't seek perfection; seek preparation and begin the journey. And don't worry about feeling nervous. Nerves and excitement feel the same when you have prepared well.

What if you think you can't make it to the finish line? No one starts something they don't believe they can finish. Most of the time, we can see ourselves completing something before we start. The challenge is that you only know your memories of the past, and that past has only taken you to where you are NOW. So, to get to a new place, you need new knowledge. Many people don't start because they feel the odds are stacked against them. But I can tell you this: you beat 50% of the people just by showing up. You will beat 40% of the people by just having a great attitude. And the last 10% is something you have to fight for. A goal-based system will set you apart and move you into the group of high achievers. All it takes is action and a good system. It doesn't matter how smart you are; unless you take action on a good system, reaching your goals and staying there will be difficult. Learning is good, but don't get stuck there. It is like having a library full of books you don't read. It is a waste. It is like owning a plane you never start, choosing to walk, and wondering why you're having problems crossing the ocean. That's not the way people cross oceans. Learning is important, but action is the key ingredient!

Action is the antidote to procrastination. Take action. Get in the habit of taking action. Become a person of action and decisiveness. It starts with making a decision and taking action on it. Many people give me the excuse that it is hard to start. Everything in life is hard to start. But once it gets going, the momentum develops. A train is hard to start but also hard to stop once it is moving.

And failure is going to happen many times on the road to success. Don't be scared of failure. Be scared of not learning from the failure and repeating the same mistakes. Once you give yourself permission to fail, you will have the courage to do anything. Don't stay in the comfort zone. The comfort zone is the failure zone. People either survive in the jungle of life or exist in the zoo, the failure zone. And if you think trying is difficult, wait until you find out what it costs you not to try.

So many people want to learn all the lessons and develop all the skills before they start. Now, you must prepare as best you can, but the secret is to get started and learn the lessons that give you the skill. You will get the lesson according to what level you are on in life. You may know you need a particular skill, but life will give you some lessons after year one. Others in year three. And other lessons may be given to you right before you reach your goal. These are the final-level skills. Lessons and skills come at the different levels of life you have graduated to.

An old African American saying goes, "If the mountain were smooth, you wouldn't be able to climb it." Expect your journey to have hard times. However, everyone on this planet is going to have hard times. Hard times are part of life. You might as well be on the side of life that wins. Climbing a mountain is hard, but being a mountain climber is the best because the best prizes are at the top. Be brave, and if you are scared, do it while being afraid because dreams become reality after thoughts become action!

Hard Work

Once you have decided, then it is time to get to work. And yes, the work is hard. Why? The greater you want your reward to be, the greater you must become. That means the future "you" may take much longer to develop than somebody else who doesn't want that much in life. One person just wants their bills paid, so they don't want that much out of life. If they don't want much, they don't have to become much. They can get one or two jobs to pay their bills and be happy. But if they want something big, their development must also be big.

So, what is it about hard work that makes people so excited? Working hard makes you look busy, whether your work is taking you towards your goals or not. However, trying harder is not the formula for success. It is the formula for exhaustion. So many people are frustrated because they are trying hard on a personal system they did not correctly design to reach their goals. And some people are stuck in life because they have not set up their system to take them anywhere. Don't get me wrong. Hard work is necessary, but doing hard work does not automatically take you to your goals because you could be working hard on the wrong things. However, hard work on your goal-based system will pay off in the future. Laziness pays off now. It is a waste of time to get mad at the results you got from the work you did not do in your system. However, the magic you seek is in the work you are avoiding.

You will never be more than you demand of yourself. If you want a clue that you are not on the path to greatness, just listen to make sure you never say you are bored. There is too much work to do to be bored. Have you ever heard people say, "I'm bored"? Boredom is a child's game. No mature person says, "I'm bored." There is too much to do in this short life to be bored. Eliminate that word from your vocabulary if you want to graduate to the next grade of life.

By doing hard work, you will develop into a stronger person with a good work ethic. But don't let hard work be your goal. Learn a new skill and renew your mind. And don't learn just to become smart and have knowledge. *Make sure your learning always leads to action.* If it doesn't, I would be very cautious about that learning. And you have to do more than give it a try. Remove the word "try" from your vocabulary. People who give up tend to use the word try all the time. Change your words from "I'll try" to "I will!"

You have to become a special key to get the best goals. So, decide now if you will be the best or not. Being average is so hard because there is so much competition. Almost everyone does just enough to be average. But the higher you go, the less competition you have. And when you get to the top, or the best of the best, because you have become one of the best, there is no competition. Since there are so few at the top, these people seek cooperation.

Don't seek to be average. Seek to be the best. That is so much easier when you get there.

Sacrifice

It is going to take sacrifice to build and execute your system daily. The tricky thing about getting your goals by sacrificing is that you feel the pain of the sacrifice many more times than the thrill of the payoff. The payoff comes once, but the pain may come hundreds of times. You have to commit right now to have a better life and accept the thousand days of sacrifice before you have your one day of reward. It may seem unfair, but systems are not about being fair. The reality is that none of it is fair, but what is sacrifice if it does not hurt? Anybody can have a better life if they build a better system. Accept the pain of sacrifice and daily discipline because your payoff comes with a big reward!

There is a saying, "How you do anything is how you do everything." That is because every action in your life is connected. Not doing your best affects your mind and your beliefs. You start to think you are not a person who follows through on the promises you make to yourself. However, if you start with small things and turn those disciplines into great disciplines, you can build confidence and trust in yourself because how you do anything is how you do everything. It is all connected. Nothing stands alone. If you want to shine in front of everybody, you must work in front of nobody.

Don't try to have less problems in your life. That is not the answer. The road to success is paved with problems. Instead of wishing for fewer problems, wish for more skills to handle the problems. Jim Rohn used to say, "Don't wish it was easier. Wish you were better!" Don't wish for less problems. Instead, become a problem solver. Successful people look at a problem and see an opportunity. Unsuccessful people run the other way. Wishing for fewer problems is like a track star running a race and wishing everyone else was slower. The track star trains until they become faster. Wishing life was easier is like wishing for less heat from an oven when baking a cake. The sacrifices are worth it in the end, not the beginning. And as you are sacrificing, be flexible. Anything that will not bend will break under pressure.

Guard Your Circle

Show me your friends, and I will show you your future. Just to have a conversation with someone, we will have to agree on certain parts of reality. To debate with someone, you must disagree on certain parts of reality. Relationships are complicated until you accept that you have different realities. The relationships in your everyday life help determine how you see the world. When you spend enough time around someone consistently over time, you begin to take each other's words, speech patterns, and beliefs because for two people to walk together, they must share a common vision. So choose wisely. There is a saying that if you take your five closest friends and average what they make a year, it will be close to what you make a year. The same thing goes for all areas of your life. You are typically the average of your closest friends. Mark Twain famously said, "Don't wrestle with pigs. You'll get dirty, and the pigs will like it. And don't argue with idiots. They will only drag you down to their level and beat you with experience." Guard your circle and choose your friends wisely. A Turkish proverb says, "When a clown moves into a palace, he doesn't become a king. The palace becomes a circus." So, I say again to guard your circle and choose your friends wisely.

Assignment: Pain and Frustration

Pain can hold you back. Write down your pain. What are the three most significant life events that still make you cry or angry like it just happened? Write them down. We do this because some life events may hold us back from where we are trying to go. Sometimes, pain takes so much energy that it robs us of the energy we need to move forward. Next, take the necessary steps to overcome that pain. I am a big believer in counseling. However you choose to address the pain, I recommend doing so before that pain shows up in your life unexpectedly, like an unwanted guest at the doorstep of your home. **Pain is inevitable, but misery is optional.**

Frustration is a matter of perspective. It is all about how you look at a problem. If somebody cuts you off in traffic, you could get mad at the driver or be happy that you are not around the driver anymore. So, it is all about how you look at the problem. That helps determine your mood, and your mood helps determine your actions. Get a better mood and perspective, and your actions will improve. Remember, optimism is the lubricant that keeps your engine going.

Self-Discipline of Consistency and Progress

What is discipline, and what does it take to get it? Discipline is one of the most important characteristics I learned on the road to achieving my goals. It is a muscle that can only get strong through resistance like any other muscle. Self-discipline is about doing the hard work now to enjoy the rewards later. Self-discipline is doing what you are supposed to do when you are supposed to do it the way it is supposed to be done. Can you make yourself do what you are supposed to even though you don't want to do it?

If there is something you know you shouldn't be doing that you want to do, can you keep yourself from it? That is discipline.

How much self-discipline do you have? Knowing you can develop a system to get more is good. How do you develop self-discipline if you do not have it? Start with one or two daily actions you will commit to. I suggest writing your daily tasks at the beginning of the day. Commit to doing this discipline. No matter what happens, you will be determined to make it happen. After a week, add another discipline designed to take you toward your goal. Keep adding and committing. It will turn you into a person with self-discipline.

An important thing to keep in mind is that consistency takes discipline, and progress takes consistency. Failure in consistency has destroyed more restaurants than bad food. Consistency helps with direction, and direction is more important than distance. Learn the difference between moving towards your goal and being busy. Many people I have advised were very busy, but they were doing busy work that was not taking them towards their goals. They were running in place really fast and never getting anywhere. We call that person a busybody. The busybody feels good about being busy, but they never get ahead because none of their busy work is taking them towards their goals. They have consistent movement but no consistent system to achieve their goals.

As you move through this journey with consistency, also move with confidence and intention in your goal-oriented system. People will respond by treating you like a serious person. People react to what they see. At a fancy restaurant or hotel, even the most disrespectful people make sure to change their behavior to match that environment because human behavior is influenced by their environment (Tuomainen & Candolin, 2011). They may not change as a person, but it is human nature to align with your surroundings. Show them greatness, and you will be surprised by how greatly people will start treating you.

So, when you are in motion, be careful not to mistake movement for progress. Both look the same, but only one helps you reach your goals in life. Some people feel so good about themselves because they are busy. I saw a guy once spend an entire day re-organizing his fishing equipment. The worst thing about it was the guy rarely went fishing. He wasted a precious day unless his goal was about relaxing; in that case, he reached his goal. It is so hard to judge someone else's journey.

If you do not consider a day precious, like water in the desert, you will pour it out on the sands of time. Protect your time. Like water in the desert, once you pour out a day, you will never get it back. The best way not to waste your time is to build a system around your day. If you don't, your days may be spent daydreaming.

That leads us to our next point. Don't let your dreams turn into daydreams by not building a system to take you there. Once you have your system, be committed to it because without commitment, you will never start, and without consistency, you will never finish. To get what you want, you have to take on the mind of a consistent person. Every consistently successful person in any particular endeavor has a system that keeps them thriving. It may just be a system for that one goal they have always wanted or their entire life, but if they accomplish goals, they are based on a goal-based system. The best companies have excellent systems. Remember, McDonald's doesn't make the best hamburgers, but they have one of the best systems. Show me your successes, and I will show you your systems. Your systems keeps you on the path to your goals because direction is more important than distance.

And if you are tired of starting over, make a commitment right now to not give up on building your goal-based system.

Keeping promises is important, but keeping promises to yourself is vital to achieve your goals. Why? When you break promises to yourself, it begins to break down your confidence in yourself. That breakdown of confidence can cause you to lose momentum on your journey to becoming the key to your success. So, what is this promise? It is a promise to carry out your system every day. By doing so, you are telling yourself that you are dependable and trustworthy. Confucius once said, "The person possessing a superior mind demands much from himself; the person with a small mind demands much from others." Demand a lot from yourself; it will help you develop into the key to your success.

The Big Picture of Delayed Gratification

When you take a picture, it is done instantly. Many years ago, the Polaroid camera made it possible for pictures to be developed on the spot, which took an extra 10 to 20 seconds. Before that, you had to take a photo to a picture developer, which took several days. Before the camera, all pictures were done by hand. If you wanted your portrait drawn, you had to sit still in the chair for hours. Delayed gratification works on the same principle.

The big picture of your life needs time to develop. That means you will have to wait for the picture of your life to develop while you're working on your system of success. Waiting for your life picture to develop may take years. We want to see the picture develop quicker than what it is. People often want your reward now, but that is not how life works. For a good example, just look outside at a tree. The tree starts as a tiny seed that can fit in your hand but can grow a hundred feet tall over the years. If you think you are more valuable than a tree, give yourself as much patience as you would a tree. Delayed gratification means putting in the work now and delaying gratification later, which takes maturity and patience. If you delay gratification, you will separate yourself from others and rise higher than you could have imagined.

Wisdom

Follow your heart, but take your brain with you. Be wise, and let others worry about being smart. What is wisdom? First, I better explain the levels of education. Information is the first level of education and happens when you are taking in facts. At this level, people accept new information that agrees with their current thinking and disregard the rest.

Once upon a time, information was hidden, so its value was high. It was all about supply and demand. Information was in short supply, so demand was high Before the spread of paper books, a few kept many of the world's secrets hidden. Then, books spread around the world (Lechêne, 2024). More people had books, so information became more available and less valuable. Next, the internet overloads us with information, so information is cheap (Schattenburg, 2007). The next level of education is knowledge. Knowledge is about knowing information (Glück, 2018). Knowledge could be knowing the subject of mathematics instead of learning the mathematical formulas. Knowing means you have a close connection with and understand the information. Information is a thing, like an object, you can know.

The highest level of education is wisdom. Wisdom is the ability to use knowledge to make good decisions and judgments (Glück,

2018). Anyone can get information. Many people can know that information. However, only a select few know how to make knowledge-based decisions. Join the top achievers and make wisdom a goal because it will allow you to keep your goals once you get them. Join the top achievers and make wisdom a goal.

Smart people know what they want. Wise people know what they don't want. Wise people know that asking better questions leads to better answers because answers hide from everything except the right questions. So, you get the correct answer if you ask the right question. If you ask the wrong question, you better prepare to write down the wrong answer. Get better at asking questions because if you do not ask, the answer will always be no. And if you ask the wrong question, the answer will always be incorrect. The smart people have heard of this principle, so they know it. The wise people know how to use this principle. Don't strive to be smart; set a goal to be wise.

And if you worry about what other people think, only worry about what you will be remembered for in life: the problems you solve and the problems you create. Use your wisdom to solve your problems. Stop looking for obstacles in every opportunity, and start looking for opportunities in every obstacle. Life is an obstacle course, so don't get shocked when you see them. That is just how life is set up. There is no hot without cold. There is no positive without negative. And there is no obstacle without opportunity.

Emotional Intelligence

Emotions are like fire. They can cook the food, or they can cook the person cooking the food. It can be the fuel that lights a fire in your heart to work for your goals, or it can burn you with a wave of anger that tears down your dreams. Learning to handle your emotions is an essential quality of a mature person. Life can hit you like an unexpected storm, but how you handle the emotions that burn inside of you is just as important. Why? If we do not control our emotions, they will take control of everything we have.

Emotions are like a forest fire. Unless we keep them contained, they will burn up everything and everyone it touches. Have you ever seen someone who cannot control their temper? They lash out at everyone, sometimes in a blind rage, and others get hurt by that rage. Controlling your emotions is a requirement for reaching your goals. When you have your emotions under control, you can make decisions that align with your goals, and alignment is crucial.

Emotions can throw us off course so slightly that it can be hard to notice. Ask anyone who has steered a boat; if you turn a boat off its course just a little, over time, you will never reach your destination. A ship with no direction never reaches its destination. But if you can persist through the emotions, taking control of your boat every time failure happens, you will achieve your goals over time. One powerful method of controlling your emotions is sight-shifting and reframing. You will learn how to do both later in this book. It is a process of understanding the problem differently to turn problems into profit.

Unless you can handle anger, you haven't got a shot. If someone can push your buttons, they can control you through emotions like anger. But why do you have those buttons in the first place? Those buttons are triggers. No one can push a button you don't have. It is your responsibility to remove those buttons you have. Those buttons will destroy your future, so you have to get them under control to graduate to the next level in the school of life.

To get them under control, we need to understand what they are. Here is what I did.

First, I wrote down what was giving me anxiety and called it "the event". Next, I wrote down the feeling. Then, I wrote down what triggered the feelings of fear when I was engaged in the activity. For example, homework used to give me anxiety. I would put it off until the last minute. After reading books on procrastination, I decided to use one of the methods. I wrote down the word homework. Next, I wrote down the feelings I associated with homework. Then, I began to write down all the reasons I was feeling fear from homework. After that, I came up with a plan to handle the event the next time it happened.

To me, homework felt like punishment. I feared looking bad in front of the teachers because I had terrible handwriting. I was also scared to admit I was a slow reader, so homework took me twice as long as the other students. I do not know if you have ever felt like that, but it is embarrassing. That embarrassment was a trigger that produced fear in me. I realized that I associated homework with fear, which gave me a fear of homework. However, I could fix each trigger once I looked at the triggers and reasons for the fear. Next, I fixed them one by one. I redefined each reason and triggered something positive. It worked for me. I made each reason fun and exciting. After that, I began to associate homework with fun. I started to like homework. It began to feel like something that would make me better instead of something that punished me. Your ability to lower the energy of emotional events the moment they happen allows you to learn from and move beyond the emotions. In contrast, others are stuck in place because of fear, anger, or sadness. Emotional control is an act of taking your power back from the event.

Assignment: Emotion Exercise System

In this next exercise, you will learn how to handle emotions. It is time to redefine your emotions to work for you instead of against you. Controlling your emotions is essential to reaching your goals. Don't worry about the future. Plan for it and turn your plans into a system. The one thing you can control is today. Worry is almost eliminated. Today affects tomorrow. Make a system to act today so you can have a better tomorrow. Let's get started.

Step 1: The Event

Write something that causes your emotions to take over. We will call it "the event". It is good to give things a name. Names help us identify people, places, things, and ideas.

Event: _____

Step 2: Event Feeling

How does it make you feel? Write down the feeling you associate with the event.

Event Feelings: _____

Step 3: Energy Level

On a scale of 0 to 10, how strong is the emotional energy you feel? A score of 0 is feeling nothing, and a story of 10 is being overwhelmed with emotion.

Energy Level: _____

Step 4: Reactions

How do you react to the event in step 2? Do you get quiet, yell, throw things, etc? List all of your reactions.

Reactions: _____

Step 5: Reason

Why did these emotions trigger you? You may find that it has something to do with past trauma or feelings. Whatever the reason, write it down. Be very honest with yourself at this moment.

Reason: _____

Step 6: Redefining the Reason

Redefining is the part of the process where we take control of the reason. Write down the benefits of the event and a new feeling for the benefits. If the event is "Someone lied to me again!" the first thing you could do is to take 30 seconds to breathe and then look for the benefit of the situation. A benefit could be this: "At least I know this now before I spent ten years being their friend." The goal in this step is to believe in the new benefit and feeling until it becomes a reality. Once you write it, you will need to say it any time the negative event happens.

Redefining the Reason: _____

Event: _____

Event Feelings: _____

Triggers: _____

Reason: _____

Redefining the Reasons: _____

You will be amazed by what you can learn from studying your emotions and finding solutions. Whenever you are feeling anxious, use this process to help you take power over your emotions. You may not be able to solve all of them, but you could free yourself up from many.

Ultimately, you realize you are not your emotions; you just feel them. Becoming emotionally aware of what events trigger you is an important quality of any leader. And we all should want to be leaders, especially leaders of our own lives. When you can lead yourself, then you can lead others. However, you can't reach your goals if you can't lead yourself to them. You are the boat's captain, and the only way to steer your boat across the ocean is for you to take control of the wheel. It is your boat, and if you do not steer it with a goal-based system, you will end up shipwrecked on an island of disappointment or floating endlessly in a sea of regret. However, if you take control of your life, you can sail your way to success.

Continue to work on mastering your emotions. I recommend reading the book Emotional Intelligence by Daniel Goleman for a deeper understanding of this subject. The way you handle disappointments is one of the measurements of maturity. Maturity does not come with age; it is developed. Maturity comes with responsibility. It starts with accepting responsibility for your words, actions, and attitudes. Another way to handle mistakes is to avoid repeating them. When you repeat a mistake, it is not a mistake anymore; it's a decision. Those mistakes and old habits do not open new doors.

Coping Mechanisms for Stress

How do you cope with stress as you are carrying out your system? Some people fold under the pressure and get depressed, while others turn to alcohol, drugs, or other addictive substances. Regardless of your coping mechanism, I am in favor of counseling to help address addiction and depression. I do not give advice on matters best suited for a licensed professional counselor. However, I will share some ways to cope with the pressures of life that have worked for me. These coping skills are much cheaper than many addictions and will save you hundreds of thousands of dollars in medical bills in the future. It will also add years to your life. On the next page, there are several ways listed that can help you handle the stresses of life.

Ways to Help with Stress

- Healthy Eating: Eating different kinds of fruits, vegetables, lean meats, and whole grains can help you feel better and stay healthy. Avoid alcohol and illegal drugs.

- Regular Exercise: Doing at least 30 minutes of physical activity most days can help lower your stress.

- Sleep: Aim for 7-9 hours of sleep each night. Keeping a regular sleep schedule can improve the quality of your sleep, which is essential for managing stress.

- Meditation: meditation can help you concentrate on the present, which can reduce anxiety. Set aside time for activities you enjoy, like reading, gardening, or listening to music.

- Talk About It: Sharing your feelings with trusted friends or family can help you feel better. I also suggest talking with a licensed professional counselor.

- Acceptance: Understanding that stress is a normal part of life can help you handle it better. Accepting stress instead of fighting it allows you to manage it more effectively.

- Positive Reframing: Look at stressful situations differently, focusing on the good things or lessons you can learn. We will discuss reframing in Chapter 8.

I encourage you to find healthy ways to deal with stress because your journey to your goals will have stressful times. That is how life works. However, even if you do nothing, you will be stressed because life is stressful. It is better to learn how to handle the stress so it does not take control of you. Next, we will learn about a specific type of stressful person, the self-proclaimed motivator.

De-motivation

Have you ever had somebody just take the motivation out of you, like taking the air out of a tire? Instead of motivating you, they demotivate you. They may have been trying to motivate you but don't know what motivates you. On top of that, they may be bad at motivating people. Their motivation sounds like this:

- The Negative Reinforcer: You are so lazy. What's wrong with you?

- The Comparer: You will never be as good as your older sibling unless you try harder.

- Reverse Psychologist: If you don't think you can, just quit.

- The Guilter: All your grandmother wanted was for you to attend college.

- Crabs in a Friend Barrel: Do you think you are better than us?

Although some may call this motivation, this type of negative reinforcement causes demotivation. We all need to know what it is, how to address it, and how to recover from it.

Demotivation happens when someone has reduced or no motivation, interest, enthusiasm, or drive. The demotivation this book addresses occurs when somebody is attempting to use negative motivation that does not work. Demotivation has the root word "demote" in it. If you are demoted in the military, you lose rank and receive a lower position. You are pushed down to a lower position if you are demoted from a job. Sometimes, people try to motivate somebody and end up making that person less motivated because of their words and actions. Whatever somebody's intention, they could hurt you and leave you scarred for life. It is common to carry the hurt from people's demotivation tactics for years.

Why Do People Demotivate?

I talk to many parents and professors who demotivate the people they are trying to help. But why do they demotivate? Sometimes, people don't know how to give advice without being negative or attacking you. Also, some of these demotivators grew up with a parent who just yelled or made them feel bad about themselves. Sometimes, people demotivate out of fear because they fear you will go down the wrong path. Some people are jealous of what you are doing because they did not accomplish their goals, so they try to live out their goals through you, but inside, they are yelling at themselves. Everyone has a reason for their actions but rarely thinks they hurt you.

The first thing to do is separate the motivation from the demotivation, and this happens by finding the truth in what they are attempting to do from the lies. How do you address a demotivator? Once you have learned from and recovered from somebody's demotivation, you are better prepared to address that person. Let the demotivator know you heard their concerns and understand why they are attempting to motivate you. And with the system you're developing in this book, you can tell them you have a plan to get your life on track and are actively working that plan out. You can let them know that they don't have to continue motivating you the way they are.

What happens if they do not stop the motivation tactics? Let them know how you are receiving their demotivation. Tell them if their demotivation makes you feel threatened, bullied, abused, bribed, not good enough, neglected, criticized, shamed, unloved, ignored, or any other negative emotion. Next, focus on the coping mechanisms discussed earlier in this chapter to relieve the stress of demotivation. And then, work on your *Upgrade Your Life* system. If your system is good enough, most people will stop trying to demotivate you because they see you are serious about reaching your life goals. Another tactic is to let them know what motivates you. A great life hack is to teach people how to treat you, and then the only way to treat you incorrectly is by choice. Sometimes, people are so harmful that they will never stop demotivating because they live in a world of demotivation. Whenever I encountered these people, I made a plan to remove myself from their influences and attacks. Whatever your plan is, make sure to stay focused on your goal-based system.

Opportunities in Disguise

Life will always present you with a series of opportunities disguised as problems. You are the key to your success, but people often become their worst enemies because they cannot control their emotions. However, when they get control, the world opens up for them, and it will do the same for you when you take control of your emotions. You can even take it a step further by addressing events from the inside instead of the outside. Capture every negative thought and call it an event. Then, follow the emotional exercise system to take control of your thoughts.

When you take control of your thoughts, you take control of your mind and take your power back. No longer are thoughts allowed to roam free and torment your mind. You are about to walk into the room of your mind and take control of your thoughts because you are the captain of your ship. You are the leader of your life, and the *Upgrade Your Life* system will help you by teaching you how to see beyond where you are so you can lead yourself beyond your limitations. The biggest challenge many people face is seeing beyond their environment and circumstances. In Chapter 8, **Meet a Real-Life Sight-Shifter!,** you will learn the secrets behind this emotional exercise system and how to take those secrets to propel your life! But first, we must take you on a journey to learn about yourself.

CHAPTER FIVE

It's Time to Face the Mirror.

All of us are self-made, but only the successful will admit it. (Earl Nightingale)

The truth is that all of us are self-made, but only the successful will admit it. So, it is time to find out what you are made of. There are a few reasons you should know what you are made of. The first one is to prevent you from getting hurt. Life can hurt if you are not careful. For example, you do not want to fly across the ocean in an airplane only to realize you did not prepare enough fuel for the trip. You have to find out so you can prepare. The following reason is to improve your weak areas. Imagine someone getting ready to run the 100-meter hurdles without knowing their jumping skills were not that good. Knowing your weaknesses lets you know exactly how to improve and what races to avoid. The last reason is to know your strengths because it lets you know what you are capable of. Imagine you walked for 10 hours through the desert to get 2 gallons of water for your house. You return home, worn out from the heat. As you open your garage, you discover a car with keys on the dashboard. You could have driven to the store the whole time. You have to know your strengths so you can make use of them. Take time to think about all of your strengths. Once you look at them, you may find out you have more skills and value than you ever realized. You will get the chance to write down those strengths and weaknesses in a couple of pages.

Your Best Average

There is a saying that goes, "Amateurs practice until they get it right, but professionals practice until they can't get it wrong." You are not judged on your best. You are judged on your average. Your average is whatever skill you have that you can do consistently every time. If you play in a basketball game and score 50 points but typically score 6 points a game, your average is not 50; it is 6 points. That is the number you can depend on. The 50-point game was just a lucky day, but it is not how you consistently do over time. The goal is to improve your average. Develop into a better player and raise your average from 6 to 10 points a game in the game of life. Over time, your average may rise to 20, and then you and everyone around you know we can depend on you to score 20 points a game. **When listing your strengths and skills, think about your best average rather than your best ever.**

Your best is not enough to win the Game of Life. What you want to focus on is your *best average.* Your best is not good enough because you can never depend on your best. You can only watch your best get lucky. Champions do not rely on luck. True champions rely on their best average. In sports, they look at your best overall average score per game. Sales managers look at your average over the year, not your best sales day. Your average is what wins the game of life. Chasing Perfection won't win your games. Raising your best average wins the game. Chasing your best average is driving you to be better every day over time, and that builds consistency. What you do on average in everyday life is what makes champions. Your best average is the key to your success.

Strengths and Weaknesses

Wouldn't it be great to know your strengths and weaknesses? When you know and can clearly express them, you are ready to design a life that works for you. Besides, do you just want to take what life gives you? Wouldn't it be better to create the life you want, just like someone would design the house they will live in? It is time to take inventory of your strengths and weaknesses. For this, you will need to take notes on your phone, computer, or any other device that allows you to take notes.

THE POWER ZONE: Your strengths and skills are known as your *power zone*. When you are operating in your power zone, you can reach your goals faster. Incorporate your power zone into the goals you create in this book.

Assignment: Strengths and Weaknesses

Step 1: Write down your top five strengths (what you are good at and all your skills). Sometimes, it takes a while to answer this. However, if you want your life to change, discover your strengths. It could be the start of what turns it all around for you.

Step 2: Write down one problem each of your five strengths can solve for people, companies, or the world. For example, you may be good at communicating. Companies need people who can communicate well to sell products or create advertising and pay a lot of money for people with those skills.

Step 3: Write down five areas of your life that you want to improve.

Step 4: For each area of improvement, write down the actions you can take every day to improve.

Every month, you should look at your strengths and weaknesses and update them. Build a system to improve the areas in need of improvement. If you need to improve your communication and public speaking skills, build a system of study and improvement in that area. The biggest mistake people make in communication is thinking that it happened. If you are a person who lies a lot, create a system that forces you to ask if being a liar aligns with who you are becoming. All actions out of alignment with the key you are becoming will slow down the whole process of becoming the key to your success. But what about all those skills and strengths you have? Put all of your skills to work in your systems to help you get to your goals. You may be more powerful than you realize. Congratulations! You are on your way to a better life!

Assignment: Money in the Bank

Wouldn't it be great to know how much money you had before you went to buy something? Have you ever made a budget? When you do, you will find out where you spend your money. Next, write down everything you spend money on in a money journal.

I was surprised when I added up how much money I spent on pistachios a year. I bought a $10 bag once a week. That means I spent $520 a year on pistachios. I never knew how much money was spent on a snack.

My coworker was living in some bad apartments because he did not have the money to stay in apartments that were $200 more a month. So, we looked at his spending in his habit-based system. We found out he spent $9 a day on Starbucks coffee and a muffin five days a week at Starbucks, which added up to $2,340 a year. $2,340 divided by 12 months is $195 a month. He discovered he could move into a better apartment if he gave up Starbucks! Until you track your expenses, you can never take control of your money. Track your money for one month and write down where your money goes. It has the power to fix money problems.

Assignment: Time-Wealth Journal

Whatever you do, you soon become what you are doing. (Bishop Malcolm Coby, Ph.D.)

Adding up what you spend your time on will tell you what you are becoming. Everyone gets 24 hours in a day. Time is so valuable. It is more valuable than gold. How do I know? If a rich person had to give up all their money to live one more day, they would pay the price. They just want one more day with their family. The fact that you are reading this book means you have a wealth of time that is more valuable than all the money in the world. Like money, every second of the day is time you have spent. Only you know if the time you spent was equal to the value of the time given. Here is an example:

- Let's say your time is worth $100 an hour. You realize that from 3:00 to 5:00 p.m., you are on social media. $100 x 2 hours = $200. That means it costs you $200 to watch social media. You have just wasted $200 and got nothing for it.

Until you track your time, you can never take control of your life because life requires time. I suggest tracking your time for one month to determine where your time is going. You will be amazed with how much time you have to work with. So, where does all your time go? Let's make a Time Wealth Journal and see.

Step 1:

Make a list of everything you do during the day. Choose one day a week. I promise you will be surprised at how much time you give freely to things that do not matter.

Include small things such as getting ready for school, preparing for work, chores, etc.

Include essential things that will help you achieve your goals, such as going to school, sleeping, spending quality time with family and friends, working, and creating a business.

Include things that do not help you achieve your goals or can lead you in the opposite direction, such as spending time on your phone talking about nothing important, non-goal-related social media, playing video games, watching sports, watching movies, etc.

Step 2:

Add all the time up and subtract that time from 24 hours. It will tell you how much time you have left during the day.

Step 3:

Take the time you have left over and the time you spent on things that were noted as necessary and add them up. It tells you how much time you have wasted. It may add up to 4 hours a day. If the wasted time is an example of your average day, multiply that by 52 weeks in a year. That equals 208 hours a year. That is 8.7 days a year that have been wasted. Many people in this world would give anything for just one more day. Wasting 8.7 days a year is shocking.

I remember being shocked when I first created a Time Wealth Journal. If you are not shocked after completing your journal, you are probably already successful and do not need to continue reading this book. If you are shocked, you need to continue reading this book because your life may depend on it.

Gratitude Wealth List

Your Gratitude Wealth List focuses on what you have going for you. Don't focus on what is missing in your life so much that you forget all the important things there. In reality, you must acknowledge what is there for something to be missing. You have a wealth of things going for you. Don't focus on lack; focus on what you have to work with because what you focus on grows. Soon, you will have more because of what you are focusing on. This focus takes gratitude. Gratitude keeps you focusing on what you have and has the added benefit of keeping you from focusing on what you lack. We all have lack and abundance, but which one do you want more of? Focus on that which you want more of.

Most people go through life without ever thinking about all they have to be grateful for. However, if you take the time to write them down, your mind, like a super-computer, will create ways to use your gratitude wealth list to help you achieve what you want in life. It is good to know all the amazing things you have to be grateful for. You may be grateful for the ability to do complex math in your head or to speak more than one language. But if you think that is all, you are missing out on some of the most valuable parts of life.

First, you are here on this earth, which is major. So many people did not wake up this morning. Being alive should be number one on your list every day. Be grateful for that. Breathing is something to be grateful for. Did you know thousands of people in the world have to use a machine or an oxygen tank to breathe? The ability to think is another great one everyone reading this book should write down. Did you know thousands of people cannot fully use their minds due to brain injury, comas, or cognitive disabilities? Your gratitude list reflects what you value in life, and to be successful, you have to keep what you value at the center of every decision.

Assignment: Gratitude Wealth List

Now, you will have the opportunity to write down a gratitude list. There is only one step. Write down at least 20 things you are grateful for. Include details about:

- Health
- Skills
- Family
- Physical abilities
- Electricity, running water, and heat
- Education

- Faith

- Anything you can think of to be grateful about

I recommend reading and updating your Gratitude Wealth List once daily. I know many successful people who do this every day. The more you do this, the more riches you will discover. Now that you know more about yourself, it is time to find out what you want. It is time to write down your goals.

CHAPTER SIX

What Do YOU Want?

If you don't know where you are going, any road will take you there. (Lewis Carroll)

This chapter is about setting goals, and you have to set goals if you are serious about your life. Setting goals is like taking a trip. You at least want to know where you are going so you can prepare for the trip. Imagine someone taking a trip without knowing where they are going. You end up going in circles or on a road to nowhere fast. Other people begin to notice your lack of direction and treat you differently. People treat you according to how they see you living your life. If you know where you are going, then you have a sense of direction in life. The beginning of any journey is to find out where you want to go. In other words, what do you want? What are your goals?

In this section, you will set goals by defining the results or changes you want to happen in your life. I am not saying you do not already have goals. I want to point out that some people have such terrible goals that the effect is bad. So, rule number one on goals is that your goals are affecting you. Your goals are things you want to have, things you want to accomplish, or issues you want to solve. Goals have to be set if you ever want to possess them. Start with a desired goal, and then the *Upgrade Your Life* system will develop a system around it. Commit to the system and the goal. After you have built your system, desire the goal and focus on the system.

Later in this book, you will learn how to change your life by changing what you see. This sight-shifting technique is the system that will help you develop the sight you need to see new paths to your goals. It will help you see the world in new ways and design a system for your life rather than just hoping things will work out. Hoping is not enough. Everyone in this world hopes. If two teams compete with each other in a sport, both teams hope they are going to win, but only one does. Even people who don't have any money hope things will happen. That should tell you something. Life does not get better by hope. It gets better by design. It is time to design a goal-based system to reach your goals.

Assignment: Discovering Your Goals

So, what do you want? Whatever you want is what we will call "goals". Build a system for goals in all areas of your life. To build your system, you must start by designing goals for every area of your life. First, what are the areas of your life? The essential areas for most successful people are family, health, finances, career, education (diplomas, degrees, certifications, and lifelong learning), and social circles (friends and your network).

In this first activity, write down your goals. Make sure to include all the important areas of your life. If not, you may end up like the company that built a beautiful house but forgot to add plans for a roof. Addressing every area will help you have a balanced life. Some people do not even have goals, and some people have goals, but they are so poorly defined they couldn't recognize them if those goals were staring them in the face. I am not condemning people who do not have well-defined goals. Just don't let that be you. Have a well-defined list of goals and start your journey to building a system for success in life.

The Need for Change: The Five Whys

To set a goal, you must know what caused you to want that goal. Five Whys is a method of solving problems by discovering what is causing them. Your goals are things you want to have, things you want to accomplish, or issues you want to solve. Sakichi Toyoda, who started Toyota Industries, created the Five Whys method. The Five Whys method has many advantages. It helps leaders identify the main reason for a problem. This method shows how one issue can lead to other problems. It also allows us to see how different reasons are connected without needing complicated ways to evaluate them (Mcaveni & Chou, 2017). We will use this approach to solve problems and set goals.

The Five Whys method involves asking the question "why" up to five times. Each time you ask "why," you dig deeper into the problem to find its cause. Once you discover the root cause, you can come up with solutions to stop the problem from happening again. These solutions become goals in the system you are developing in this book. This method is simple but works well. It includes these steps:

1. Clearly explain what the problem is.

2. Ask "why" several times to understand the root cause.

3. Create solutions to fix the problem.

The following is an example of the Five Whys method. Notice how each answer becomes the next question.

The Problem	The machine stopped working
1. Why did the machine stop?	Because the fuse blew due to an overload.
2. Why was there an overload?	Because the bearings weren't lubricated enough.
3. Why weren't they lubricated enough?	Because the lubrication pump wasn't pumping enough.
4. Why wasn't it pumping enough?	Because the pump shaft was worn and rattling.
5. Why was the shaft worn out?	Because there was no filter to keep metal scraps out.
Root Cause	There was no filter to keep metal scraps out.

Assignment: Root Cause of Being Late to Work

This practice example takes a problem and has you ask why enough times to find the root of the problem. On the second row, ask why about the first reason given for the problem. On the next row, ask why about the reason given for the first why. Keep going until you get to the 5th Why. The 5th one is the most likely root cause of the problem.

The Problem	Being Late for Work
Why?	
Why?	
Why?	
Why?	
Why?	
Root Cause	

Assignment: Root Cause of the Expensive Shoes

Now, let's find the root cause of expensive shoes. On the second row, ask why about the first reason given for the problem. In the next row, question the reason given for the first why. Keep going until you get to the 5th Why. The 5th Why is the most likely root cause for buying expensive shoes.

The Problem	Buying Expensive Shoes
Why?	
Why?	
Why?	
Why?	
Why?	
Root Cause	

Assignment: Root Cause of a Problem You Are Having

Now, write down something you want in the first row of the right column. On the second row, ask why about the first reason given for the problem. On the next row, ask why about the reason given for the first why. Keep going until you get to the 5th Why, which is the most likely root cause of your problem.

The Problem	
Why?	
Why?	
Why?	
Why?	
Why?	
Root Cause	

Now you know the root cause of your problem, you can set a goal to fix it.

Assignment: Root Cause of Something You Want

Now, write down something you want in the first row of the right column. On the second row, ask why about the first reason given for the problem. On the next row, ask why about the reason given for the first why. Keep going until you get to the 5th Why. The 5th Why is the most likely root cause of why you want what you want.

What Do You Want?	
Why?	
Why?	
Why?	
Why?	
Why?	
Root Cause	

You can set a better goal now that you know the root cause of what you want. The 5th Why is the most likely root cause for your problems or goals. If the answer supports your goals in life, then you know that what you want is worth going after. Discovering the root cause of the issue is the power of the Five Whys. Whether your goal is to fix a problem or go after a goal, use the Five Whys to discover the need for change.

Assignment: Future Self

It is time to find out who you want to be. Describe the version of the "future you" you want to become. The only things you need to describe in this section are the characteristics of the person you want to be. As you are on your journey to your goals, you want to know if you are becoming the person you want to be. You can use descriptions like kind, strong, happy, a person who gives to charity, etc. Finish the statement below by adding several words or phrases to describe the person you will be when you reach your goals.

When I have reached all my goals, I will look in the mirror and see a person who is:

Now you know the kind of person you want to be. You can begin to make goals that align with your future self.

Assignment: Make a List of Goals.

You should be able to tell people your goals in life as confidently as you tell someone your favorite brand of car or favorite foods. To be successful in this world at a high level, make sure that what you want is connected to a big problem you can solve for a large group of people. Find the big need and become the big solution. Impact drives income. How you impact other people determines your income. Later in the book, when you make your system, you may be surprised to see the connections between your strengths, goals, and solutions that can solve big problems for a large group of people (corporations, hospitals, etc.), which will save you from wasting time. You have a small space in this book for your goals, but write your goals somewhere else so you have more room to write. In the first column, write your goal. Write whether the goal is small, medium, or large in the second column. For the best results, create goals that cause you to operate in your **power zone**.

Goal	Small, Medium, or Big

Qualifying the Qualified

As you set your goals, you need to know what it takes to be qualified to achieve them. Let's say your goal is to be a doctor who treats people with heart conditions. You would need to research the qualifications for a doctor who deals with the heart. Look at your goals and determine what you have to do to qualify for each goal. The qualifications are specific to your goals. Even if your goal is to have better relationships, the qualifications may be relationship skills, empathy, good communication skills, forgiveness, and patience. If you are missing any qualifications, develop a plan for achieving those qualifications and build those actions into your system. Once you do that, you will know exactly how long it will take to be qualified. This is going to take a lot of research to find out what it takes to be qualified. Don't rely on your own knowledge. Do your research. Below are three spaces. Write your goals in the left column, and write the qualifications needed to have the goal. Use a separate document if you needed.

Goal	Qualifications

The Bottom Line

What is your button line? You must discover when your panic button kicks in to achieve your goals. Whether your goal is a career, getting in shape, family, or finances, we all have a bottom line. For example, your bottom line is never to have under $1,000 in your bank account. If that is your bottom line, when your bank account gets to $1,200, you will panic and find opportunities to keep your money from ever getting that low. Some people have a certain weight, and that is their bottom line. When they get to that weight, they go into panic mode. That weight is unacceptable to them, and they will spend day and night working out and eating healthy foods.

Shift your field of vision to raise your bottom line. When I started performing on my guitar, I would accept jobs that pay $100. Then, I raised my field of vision to $400. Soon, I would not even think about performing for $100. My advertising began to target people who would pay $400. My field of vision shifted to only seeing things above $400 a gig. We all have a floor or a bottom number that we will never go below. For some people, that means having no less than $100 in the bank; for others, that means having no less than $100,000. Whatever that bottom line is, that is where your stress kicks in. Raise your bottom line if you want to see bigger opportunities.

Assignment: Bottom Line

So, what is your bottom line? Your bottom line is the line you reach when you need to panic because you have not reached your goals. Everyone has a bottom line, but so many people do not take the time to think about what that is. They just let life happen on autopilot until a feeling kicks in. Usually, that feeling is caused by an eviction notice or their lights getting cut off. I am not judging anyone. You had better know where your bottom-line panic button is, or your life would be one big shock! Let's figure out your bottom line. Write down three to five goals you want to set. After that, write down your bottom-line statement to tell you when you need to panic because you are not reaching your goal.

Goal 1:_____

Bottom Line 1:_____

Goal 2:_____

Bottom Line 2:_____

Goal 3:_____

Bottom Line 3:_____

Goal 4:_____

Bottom Line 4:_____

Goal 5:_____

Bottom Line 5:_____

Goal Alignment

Are your goals in opposition to each other? Are your goals in alignment with each other? Your goals pull you in their direction. If that is the case, and all your goals are moving in the same direction, then you can reach them faster. So, you must determine if your goals pull you in different directions.

The more your goals align, the more they reinforce each other. Each goal gives the other goals strength to move in the same direction. What if you were watching a bicycle race where all the bicyclists start at the same time but are facing in 20 different directions? They would quickly crash into each other.

Assignment: Goal Review

- Review your list of goals and ask yourself if they align. Here are three questions to ask yourself.

- Do your goals align with the "future you" described earlier in this chapter?

- Are your goals in alignment with each other?

- When you reach all of your goals, can each of your goals live side by side?

- Are your goals in opposition?

If your goals are not aligned, take time to modify them. If your goals contradict each other, fix them. How? Align your goals with your future self. Now that you have goals and bottom lines, it is time to add fuel to the fire. It is time to find your reasons for going after your goals. It is time to find those powerful reasons for *Upgrading Your Life*. Go to the next chapter to give power to your goals.

CHAPTER SEVEN

Find Your Motivation and Win!

Anyone who has the 'why' to live can bear almost any 'how.'
(Nietzsche)

In this section, you will develop a list of reasons for achieving your goals. How motivated are you to change something in your life? Well, your reasons are your motivation. If you can find enough reasons to do something, you can get yourself to do anything. Everyone has reasons for doing anything. If you don't believe me, go up to someone and ask them to walk across the street. The first thing then will say is, "Why?" Ask a kid to look out the window, and they will ask. "Why?" They want to know the reason. Throughout human history, people have died in wars for powerful reasons (Baard et al.. 2014; Levy, 1998). Every heroic act a superhero does has been done for a reason. A person with a good enough list of reasons can do anything. Reasons make the difference in the results you want. If the reason is powerful, getting it done will be much easier.

I once knew a person who went to medical school because they lost their mother to a preventable disease. This person wanted to find a way to save other families from a loss that could have been prevented if they had been able to visit a doctor. Her reason was so powerful she didn't need another reason. Another person became a lawyer because she was denied a job in her younger years because of her race. It was a reason that kept her up all night studying. Her reason fueled the fire she needed to keep going. She had a powerful reason to finish law school.

Are your reasons powerful enough to take you on the hard journey to your goals? What if your big reason is to make the communities safe for kids because yours was not? Maybe you want to find a cure for cancer because you lost your grandmother to this deadly disease. There is a reason for everything. Why do you keep coming back to school or work? Day after day, you are here. Is it to change your future and make it better? When you understand why, you can make the most of those reasons. Those reasons can launch you like a rocket!

There are so many possibilities around you, and you can learn to maximize all of them. If your reasons for doing something are strong enough, taking action is much easier. It is about getting powerful enough reasons. So many people get started and quit. I am sure you know people like this. I know people like this. I have been one of those people. So, getting started is good, but it is not enough. You have to have the fuel to stay in the race. You have to have a powerful list of reasons.

Reasons for Not Doing Well

So many people have reasons for not doing better in life. We have all heard the reasons: It's too hard; I am too tall, too short, too young, too old, etc. The one I hear the most is, "Everybody is against me." Really? Everybody. You would be surprised how little the world thinks about you. With 8 billion people on the planet, the world cannot spend its whole time being against any one person. So, don't mistake excuses for reasons; make systems for getting things done. Over the years, many students have given me so many reasons why they do not want to go to college, trade school, or go into business:

- "I'm tired of learning. Twelve years in school to get a high school diploma feels like enough school for me."

- "I am scared to leave home."

- "What if I fail?"

- "What if I am not smart enough or good enough?"

- "I don't know what I want to do with my life."

- "I don't belong here."

People give me so many excuses for not to pursue their dreams. Replace your excuses with the reasons you will develop in this chapter.

Identity Crisis and the Imposter Syndrome

Let's look at one of the biggest killers of progress, the Imposter Syndrome. Have you ever felt fake in a class or that you did not deserve to belong there? Have you ever felt like you are not smart enough, especially when a standardized test says you are not smart enough to be there? You are not alone. That is the imposter syndrome talking. I remember being told in school that I was not smart enough, and my teacher said that to me! Fast-forward to now, and all those teachers have to greet me as Dr. Lee. Trust me, that is a great feeling. So remember, you do not have to be the smartest to win. Many people suffer from imposter syndrome. Sometimes, these thoughts come from your past programming talking to you. It is this voice in your head that plays negative talk all day. It can affect work, school, relationships, and anything else you are involved in.

So many people fear being discovered they are a fraud and do not deserve to be here. So, they begin to overperform to compensate for the imposter syndrome. When rewarded for their overachievement, they feel they must continue this vicious cycle. Another type of imposter syndrome is when someone does not accept compliments. They feel like they do not deserve the praise. These people often disregard the praise and point out their mistakes. If that is you, all of that is about to end. You will move past the imposter syndrome by developing an *Upgrade Your Life* goal-based system that will make you feel so powerful that you will never be the imposter again. On the road to success, this is one of the major issues you must conquer, especially the higher you climb in life. It is natural to feel like you do not belong somewhere you have never been. However, when you finish the *Upgrade Your Life* system, you will know how to overcome the imposter syndrome. After building your goal-based system, you can thank the people for the compliment because you are on a well-designed journey with a well-designed *Upgrade Your Life* system. In this book, you will build a system that will take you well beyond your limitations. You will feel unstoppable!

To develop an excellent system for yourself, you must be clear on who you are to avoid an identity crisis. An identity crisis happens when you are not living your truth. When you are living your truth and confident in who you are, you have power because identity confidence gives you power. When your identity aligns with your life goals, you develop **identity power**. This book will provide you with identity power. Doing life as you have always done is not the path to success. If doing what you've always done would work, it would have already work for you. It is time to work on something new. It is time to upgrade your identity.

Is It Time for You to Change?

The change you are looking for begins with you. For your life to change, you have to change. Change a lot if you want things to change a lot. Change a little if you want things to change a little. Just make a change. You may not notice the change with your eyes since change happens from the inside. You have to look deeper within yourself. You are designing a system to change you from the inside so you can have what you want on the outside. Make a system instead of making excuses. Make a commitment that you are going to change. Everything you're looking for in your life is only visible through the eyes of the person you need to become. Don't look for it in the way you have always lived because all you will find is what you already have. It is easy to stay the same and continue doing what you have always done, but what you have always done will only get you what you have always gotten.

Think of the events that happen in life. An example of an event is rain. You can't stop the rain from coming, but you can change how you do things by capturing it and using it to your advantage. Some people look at the rain and decide to change their yard. They dig a path to a well so they can always have water to drink. Some people don't dig a path because they do not want to change the yard, and these are the same ones who complain about being thirsty. Some people get so stubborn about digging up their old way of thinking that they drown in life's storms. It is your decision. The rainwater will flow towards whatever path you have dug for it. Water takes the path of least resistance, making digging more exciting because you have a say in how the water of your life flows. You can't stop the storms of life from coming, but you can dig the path to your well. You get to design how you want your life to flow.

Excuses

Before we discuss reasons, let's discuss reason's evil twin, excuses. Excuses are like people; they are cute when you are a little child, but when you grow up, they are no longer cute. Excuses have stopped more people on the road to success than traffic lights have stopped cars in big cities. Excuses are rarely motivation and do more harm to the garden of your life. They are the weeds in the garden that choke the life out of the goals you are planting. Here is a list of common excuses people use when they do not reach their goals.

- People don't think I am smart enough.

- I don't know the right people.

- Those people don't like me.

- I went to a bad school.

- It's too hard.

- I don't have enough money.

- I don't have the time.

Those excuses may be valid, but they do not have to stop you. Excuses are acceptable but do not carry them throughout your day. Work your best not to use excuses. Outside of the close family and friends who love you, no one wants to hear any excuses from someone older than ten. When you finish this book, you will see why these excuses do not help you. Having a system eliminates the need for excuses because they are a weak energy source and cannot power your system. If you are not careful, excuses can drain your power. So, put away all of your excuses and replace them with reasons. Your reasons are the fuel that keeps you consistently going and the energy to power the *Upgrade Your Life* system you are building.

Reasons: What Is Your Reason Level?

Why do you want your goals so bad? Do you really want them that badly? Some go after their goals because they don't want to be like their parents. Some people grew up poor and will not go back to that. Some people grew up with a sick relative and want to help heal people. Sometimes, the best reasons for doing something are for others and not ourselves. There is a story of a man who went to medical school because he lost his mother to a heart attack. His reason was so big he never gave up. Your reasons are the spark that starts your fire and the fuel that keeps you going when times get tough. Some people look for a reason to get up in the morning. Other people look in the mirror and say that is reason enough! Do you want your goals that badly? When you do, then you will be ready to start. The desire is seen in the pursuit.

Two big motivators for achieving our goals are the thrill of victory and the agony of defeat. When you win big at something, it can motivate you to have the same victory again. That is a great reason to keep going. And then defeat can be so painful that you do not want to experience that again, so you have a powerful and painful reason never to experience that defeat again. How do you want something that badly? With a strong enough list of reasons, you will know and start your journey to success.

Assignment: Reasons for Success

Step 1:

Write your list of goals you created in chapter 6.

Step 2:

REASONS: Make a list of reasons for each goal. These should be big reasons and small reasons. The list must be long enough to never run out of reasons to fuel you when you need inspiration and motivation. The reasons need to be as big and emotional as possible. Connect them to your family and other major life connections. If you want, make them mission-oriented, like inspiring children to read or saving the oceans. In the first row, write one of your goals. In the second row, list why you are going after the goal. Try to have at least five reasons for each goal. Some people have 10 or 20. The reasons will be the fuel you have to continue towards your goal. The more fuel you have, the further you can go.

Goal 1:
List of Reasons
1.
2.
3.
4.
5.

Goal 2:
List of Reasons
1.
2.
3.
4.
5.

Next, it is time to rate your reasons to determine their power. The more powerful your reasons, the more likely you are to reach your goals.

Scoring the Energy Level of Your Reason

Knowing the energy level of your reason is important because when you do not feel like continuing towards your goals or the journey gets hard and you feel like giving up, the energy of your reasons will give you the strength to keep going.

Step 1:

In the first column, list each reason for your goal. In the second column, assign an energy score from 0-10 for each reason. A score of 0 means that reason does not get you excited. A score of 10 means that reason gets you excited and motivated to start and never stop. Your energy score is a genuine emotional reaction, not just a logical reaction. How much does this reason get you excited and fired up? Write the energy level score in the second column.

Step 2:

Final Score: Add up your final score and divide it by the number of reasons you listed. Compare it to the range chart to find your motivation level. The number of reasons times total emotional energy level score = your motivation number.

Take the total and divide it by the number of reasons. Then multiply that number by 10. That total becomes the percentage.

Total Score (TS): ___

Total Number of Reasons (TNR): ___

TS ___ divided by TNR ___ = Energy Level ___

Energy Level ___ x 10 = ___%

Example

Here is an example of getting in shape. The reasons are on the left, and the emotional energy levels are on the right.

Reasons for Goal 1 - Get in Shape	Energy Level
To be around for my family	10
To get off medication	10
To run a marathon	1
To look good for the class reunion	5
To feel better on an everyday	3
To fit into my old clothes	6
Total	**35**

- Total Score: 35

- Total Number of Reasons: 6 reasons

- 35 divided by 6 reasons = 5.8 x 10 = 58%

Next, see the Emotional Energy Level Chart to determine what the score means.

Emotional Energy Level Chart

- 91-100% Can't Be Stopped

- 81-90% Extremely Motivated

- 71-80% Highly Motivated

- 61-70% Motivated

- 51-60% Almost Motivated

- 41-50% Half-Way Motivated (You have good intentions but will have trouble being consistent. Find better reasons or accept defeat.)

- 31-40% Barely Motivated (This person will start and quit in a week. Find better reasons or accept defeat.)

- 21-30% Barely Motivated (This person will start and quit in a few days. Find better reasons or accept defeat.)

- 11-20% Barely Motivated (This person will start and quit the next day. Find better reasons or accept defeat.)

- 0-10% Not Motivated (This person is not ready to change. Find better reasons or accept defeat.)

Let's look at the score. A score of 58% tells us that the reasons are enough motivation to get started but not enough to finish.

- 51-60% Almost Motivated: You have good intentions but will have trouble being consistent. Find better reasons or accept defeat.

Anything below 70% is a danger zone for any goals. Would you ever put your faith in a doctor whose motivation is only 58%? In this example, a person needs better reasons to raise their score. Otherwise, they will have a higher probability of quitting when times get challenging. It is time for you to gather your list of reasons. I will provide space for two reasons to get you started, but use another document to write more goals and reasons.

Reasons for Goal 1	Energy Level
Total	

Total Score (TS): ___

Total Number of Reasons (TNR): ___

TS ___ divided by TNR ___ = Energy Level ___

Energy Level ___ x 10 = ___%

Reasons for Goal 2	Energy Level
Total	

Total Score (TS): ___

Total Number of Reasons (TNR): ___

TS ___ divided by TNR ___ = Energy Level ___

Energy Level ___ x 10 = ___%

So many people have excuses for not going after their dreams. Excuses have a low energy level for motivating you to pursue your goals. Now, you will function on reasons instead of excuses because you need a high score to get started. Don't waste your precious time making excuses. Spend time creating big reasons that will fuel your system to success. Get a large list of reasons so you never run out of inspiration. My reasons lists usually have at least ten powerful reasons per goal and can go as high as forty. I want the energy level to be high. So, I need the power of the reasons, and I want the list to be long enough I will never run out. When you build your reasons list, you will know you are ready to start when your energy level score is over 70%. When you get over 70%, you will have the fuel and the fire you need to finish what you started.

You need many reasons to do one thing because all of your reasons will not always be at the highest emotional level at the same time. Sometimes, one will be up, and the other will be down. That is another reason you need many reasons; you can switch those out when needed and always have the fuel you need to carry on your system. Read your reasons daily and memorize them. When you need motivation and inspiration to keep doing your daily system, just pull out your list of powerful reasons.

CHAPTER EIGHT

Meet a Real-Life Sight-Shifter!

Have you ever noticed people who seem to be living a different reality than yours? It is like they see the world differently. Let me be the first one to tell you it's true! I want to reintroduce myself at this time. I am Dr. Lorne Lee, and I am a sight-shifter. I did not develop sight-shifting. It is an ancient science I have been studying for a long time, and I will share some of the secrets of sight-shifting that will help you develop your system of success. This chapter is all about shifting the way we see the world and reframing situations so you can turn your problems into profits. What if you woke up one day and found out we were all looking at the same sky but seeing something different? We see the world according to our experience and knowledge of it.

A primary key to becoming the key to your better future is how you see things, which is sometimes called your perspective. How you see the world gives you the information needed to stimulate and stir up what is inside you. Jim Rohn once said, "People are mainly affected by how they think things are more than how they are." I found that to be true. So many things are in your head, but humans have a great superpower to activate sight…words.

Words are an evolutionary step in human history. Words activate sight in our minds with sounds from our mouths (Noorman et al., 2018). If somebody says the word car, all kinds of cars appear in our minds. If someone says red car, suddenly we will see a red car in our minds. If we were at a car dealership, all the red cars would suddenly stand out from all the other cars. Words revolutionized the human experience. Next, systems of writing were developed. When writing came along, the visual symbols of the written word began to activate sight in our minds. Suddenly, humans could write down the country's entire history to activate the sight of future generations so they could see into the past.

Words add up to being our knowledge. Words can change the sight we see in our minds, but they can also change what we see with our physical eyes. Here is an example to illustrate my point. Scientists studied fear by proving that babies were not even scared of snakes when shown videos. The adults were the ones who were scared because the fear was in their minds (LoBue & Adolph, 2019). The fear the adults had came from their knowledge of snakes. The snake revealed itself to the adults as a danger in their minds. The babies had no knowledge of snakes, so the snakes appeared to be toys to the babies. The babies only knew about toys, so the snake turned into a toy in the baby's mind.

The rubber hand illusion is another study that examines how information from the eyes clashes with reality. The brain creates fake realities and feelings to understand what is happening. In the rubber hand illusion, people feel like a fake rubber hand is theirs. This effect occurs when both the actual hand and the rubber hand are stroked at the same time with paintbrushes. As this happens, the brain can sometimes change how it thinks about where the real hands are located. This change, known as proprioceptive drift, is connected to the feeling of owning the rubber hand (Rohde et al., 2011). What you think shapes how you see and experience the world.

Your thoughts are a collection of words. Words are the keys that unlock sight. Knowledge is a collection of words. If you want a new life, you need new knowledge; they can instantly change what you see. It is almost like magic. Words are an evolutionary step in human history because they create pictures in the brain. If you say "mom, dad, dog, and money," images of all four will pull up in your mind as quickly as an image search on the internet. Your ability to use new words to shift and rebrand the images in your mind is a major key to your success. If you can switch or rebrand the images in your mind, you can radically control your mind. People do it all the time but don't always have a system to get good at it. They say things like, "Look on the bright side" and "Think positive," but all those phrases are skills that must be developed. Those phrases only develop lower-level sight skills instead of the mastery-level sight that will be the key to your better future.

When you can rename and redefine what you are experiencing every moment, you can shape your reality to direct you toward your goals. That is rebranding. Companies do this all the time. Kentucky Fried Chicken rebranded itself by changing the name to KFC. McIntosh rebranded itself as Apple. Why do they rebrand themselves? So you would see them as something new with a whole new image. Doing this will teach you to shift your sight to see more at a higher level. Did you know there were higher levels of sight? There are! There is a reason a child does not see the world the same way as a person who has lived through wars, had grandchildren, and climbed up one of the highest mountains in the world. But you do not have to do all those things to raise your sight level. You can start your sight-shifting development right now. Sight-shifting is a skill that top-level people have. It is essential to the winner's toolbelt. You can develop this skill and join the top achievers of life.

The Truth About Sight

This universe we live in is stranger than many realize. According to NASA, most of the universe is beyond our sight level, but the parts of the universe we can't see are still real. 68% of the universe is made up of dark energy that is invisible to humans. It is not only unknown, but it is unknowable to the human mind. We will never be able to know it or comprehend it. 27% of the universe is made of dark matter. It is currently unknown and invisible to humans, but one day, we may know what it is. However, we will never see it. Over 5% of the universe is made of invisible interstellar space dust and visible matter (Abbott et al., 2022). So far, over 95% of the universe is invisible, but it is very real.

Just because you can't see it doesn't mean it isn't there. There is an invisible world and a visible world. Even everything that can be bought or was built first lived in the invisible world of someone's imagination, and then it was brought into the physical world by physical means. So, the invisible world is real, but to know what is real, we must move beyond our eyes to see reality. In reality,

126

we do not see with our eyes; we see with our mind. Our mind receives information from our eyes. Our mind filters that information through the lens through which we see the world. This lens is based on our knowledge, a word collection. That is why you can close your eyes and still see in your mind. If I say "cat," can you see a cat in your mind? That helps you understand that sight is in the mind. The sight mind also points out the limitations of our minds. We can only see as much as our knowledge will let us see.

Simply put, you cannot see beyond your knowledge. In one sense, we are trapped by our knowledge. Knowledge is not about how smart you are; it is all about which knowledge you know. A genius could be walking down the street clueless to the criminal activity happening on the same street. The genius may not have enough knowledge about criminal activity to spot crime. So, if you want to see more, you must learn more. This sight-shifting chapter of *Upgrade Your Life* will teach you to see more through knowledge. This book will teach you how to take control of your sight.

With every shift in human history, a change in sight soon appeared. In the early 1900s, people worked as switchboard operators at the telephone company. A caller would call the operator from their house, and the operator would transfer the call to the person the caller wanted to talk to at another house (Daughterty, 2023). When automatic switching was invented, people could connect their calls without operators. Everyone had to switch their mental sight from contacting operators to making calls on their own. Commercial flying switched the way people saw transportation. When they first developed this new knowledge of flight, they created a new sight. When they had new sight, they came up with all new possibilities. Now, we have planes flying around the world 24 hours a day.

We only see the world according to our knowledge. Imagine people standing in a crowded elevator. Everyone in the elevator is experiencing a different reality. One person is experiencing anxiety about being late for work. So the world is moving very fast to them. Another person sees they are trapped, and the walls are closing in because they are claustrophobic (a fear of being confined in small spaces). Another person thinks the elevator is about to fall because they always see the worst in every situation. They hear a noise in the elevator line and visualize the cables barely holding together. That person's heart begins to pound. Another person sees nothing but a box of candy because they are five years old and crave fun treats. Everyone is in the same elevator but is seeing different realities.

Being Trapped by Your Own Prison of Sight

When we do not know what to do, we do more of what we know. We build these mental prisons in our minds, willingly enter, lock ourselves in, and hide the key (Bolman and Deal, 1991). There was a time when my life had stopped progressing. Nothing seemed to be going right. I was frustrated and felt like my life was doomed to be stuck on replay, like a song you could not stand. Then, one day, I looked around and realized I was not stuck. I was trapped in a mental prison of my creation. I was so trapped in one way of thinking that I imprisoned myself in a place that housed all of my anger and frustration. Anyplace you stay long enough, your mind will believe it is your new home. It will hang family pictures on the wall and start decorating. My mind had made anger and frustration a new home. So, I had to become the key that unlocked the door to my mental prison. I had to trick my mind into taking on new actions and a new self-identity using sight-shifting by learning new knowledge and words. And feel free to trick your mind because your mind is always tricking you. Your mind fills in missing information to make sense of the world (Rohde et al., 2011). Countless research studies have documented this brain trick, such as the McGurk Effect of having the brain override the ears to replace words you hear, studies on the brain's ability to fill in missing information to help see and interact with objects, and the Hebbian research on the psychological and neurological underpinnings of learning (Singh et al., 2024; Papenmeier et al., 2019; Magliano et al., 2017; Milner, 2003). All are great examples of how our minds make up fake information to make sense of the world.

How Do We See?

We see according to our knowledge. Here is an example. A police officer, a firefighter, and a doctor walk into a big concert with thousands of people in the crowd. The police officer immediately sees potential crimes happening. As the crowd gets louder, the officer sees a potential Code 10-44 (a riot in progress). The police officer is also looking for possible Code 10-60 (suspicious vehicle) and Code 10-65 (armed robbery) crimes in progress. The concert reveals itself according to the police officer's knowledge. All of these codes are invisible to everyone else. The firefighter walks in and determines if the smell in the room is a possible 10-33, which can be a Code 1 or Code 2 because of the odor conditions from a potential heat source. The firefighter also notices a possible 10-31 Code 1 because of a defective sprinkler system. They can even see the water pipes behind the walls in their mind. All of this is invisible to everyone else because the people at the concert do not have firefighter knowledge in their minds.

Then, the doctor on staff at the concert walks into the room and sees someone who looks like they could be suffering from a stroke. The doctor sees the signs of a stroke and jumps into action to save the person. The room revealed itself differently according to each person's knowledge. The police officer sees the room through police knowledge. The firefighter sees the room according to the firefighter's knowledge, and the doctor sees the room according to medical knowledge. Do you think the three took different actions because of their knowledge? Of course, they did because sight affects actions. If you see the stick on the ground as a weapon to defend yourself from a dog chasing you, you will grab the stick quickly. If you see that stick is a snake, will you grab it? Probably not, because your knowledge of snakes will stop you from grabbing it.

Knowledge affects sight, and sight affects actions. If you want new actions, you must gain new sight. And if you are going to gain a new level of sight, you must acquire new knowledge. You see according to your knowledge. The police officer may miss the opportunity to save the person from a stroke because they do not have the medical knowledge to reveal the medical opportunities to them. So, if you gain new knowledge, you will see the world in new ways. Also, your new knowledge will reveal opportunities that were invisible to anyone not possessing knowledge on the level of that opportunity.

Believing Is Seeing

Seeing is not believing. Believing is seeing. You have to believe what something is before you can see it. Another way of looking at it is you only see what you believe. I once heard a parent say to a college dean, "I can't believe my son would ever do something like that!" And then, the dean showed a video of their teenager breaking school property. The parent's world was thrown upside down. They now believe their teenager could destroy school property. When they brought her son in, she looked at him differently. No longer did the mother see the sweet, innocent boy who went off to college. Now, he is a kid who destroys property. Our sight level can make us overlook objects in our environment.

Babies will overlook gold and diamonds in a sea of rocks because they do not believe in what diamonds and gold are. They are all just rocks. That is why babies treat people the same. But when they get older and understand who that person is, they can cling to one and avoid the other. That is why babies are not afraid of snakes, but most adults are. "Seeing is believing" is the formula for failure. "Believing is seeing" is the formula for success. When you learn to believe in the positive outcome you want, you will begin to see the path to that positive outcome in your physical environment.

What does your mind see? How does the brain interpret information from the eyes? How does the brain fill in details from incomplete images based on your knowledge, which is just a collection of words? Your language may be holding you back. Your sight is based on your knowledge, which is just a collection of words. Change your words and change your reality. Words activate images and stories in the mind. The word we call an object or a person develops a story around that object or person. Next, we treat that object or person according to that story. The words you say the most reflect the knowledge you have in your head. That knowledge determines the sight you see. So, your words create your reality, and you treat everything and everyone according to your reality. If you want a new reality, you need new words.

Sight-Shifting: Seeing Five Things in One Object

Upgrade Your Life is based on the ancient skill of sight shifting. The system is based on seeing multiple perspectives at one time. Here is an example. A tree becomes pressed shavings of wood, which becomes paper, then a document, and then a certificate of deposit for 1 million dollars, which becomes a means to buy a house made out of the same wood the paper is made out of. It is all the same wood. This vision-shifting exercise is an example of seeing six different levels of sight, and there are many more levels of sight. Most people can only see one thing at a time, which means they can only see on one sight level at a time. Our words are painting our realities as we speak. When you can see more, you have more options in life.

Sight-shifting is built on cognitive reframing. Cognitive reframing is a behavioral psychological technique where a person identifies and changes how situations, experiences, events, ideas, and emotions are viewed (Sharma et al., 2023). Cognitive reframing is the process that challenges and changes what is viewed. This change allows you to reframe the thought to change what you see. Reframing will enable you to think about situations from more than one point of view, which lets you create other solutions and strategies unavailable to lower sight levels (Bolman and Deal, 1991). Reframing results means having different solutions appear at different sight levels. Level one may have four solutions. Level three may have five solutions. If you can see level 7, then you have nine solutions available. You would have 18 solutions by shifting sight levels instead of the four solutions from level one. The more sight levels you can see, the more solutions you will become aware of. You become a bottomless well of solutions.

Why reframe your problems? Frames create focus, and reframing gives you the power to control your focus. Creating a new frame within a frame will change your actions by changing the emotions that drive them. In the next section, you can do a series of sight-shifting exercises to expand your vision and see more opportunities.

Expanding Your Sight

So, how do we get new sight? We learn and use new knowledge. The biggest knowledge in our minds gets our brain's attention. How do you make knowledge bigger in our brains? We use words of that knowledge because words focus our attention; think of words like a spotlight in our minds. If you start using words of nature all the time, soon you will see nature everywhere, even while everyone can't see it. The world will reveal itself to you through the lens of nature. It works for everything in existence.

Assignment: Sight-Shifting

Shifting sight levels is about developing the ability to see multiple realities for one object or person. Let's see how well you can use this modified ancient technique to alter your reality. These techniques go back thousands of years. I will compact them into quick exercises that will change your life. It is a great idea to do these exercises often. Think of them like a gym workout for your mind. The more you do them, the stronger you will get at sight-shifting.

Sight Shifting Exercise 1: Become Opportunity-Minded

The purpose of this exercise is to expand the opportunities available to you. This exercise will develop the skill of turning everything around you into opportunities. In this exercise, we will find multiple opportunities in different situations. Remember, the key to reframing is to practice regularly. The more you challenge negative thoughts and experiment with new perspectives, the easier it will become to shift your mindset. When you reframe the problem, you have a different solution. It is time to reframe your life. You will be provided with situations. For each situation, write down 3-5 possible opportunities. If you can find more, write them down. It is like the game of finding the hidden items in a picture. For example:

Situation: Every Saturday, a bus full of tourists stops directly in front of your house because you live next to a famous tree.

Hidden Opportunities:

1) Sell bottled water in front of your house, especially on hot days.

2) Offer professional picture services in front of the tree.

3) Provide chairs for people who cannot stand for a long time so they can enjoy the experience longer.

4) Be kind to someone you do not know. Get to know the people on the bus and make new friends every week.

5) Offer the bus driver free snacks if the bus driver promotes your snack stand in front of your house.

6) If the people are loud, provide meditation music near the tree to encourage people to be quiet.

Six opportunities were created based on the problem of having a tree next to a house. It is your turn. I will provide the two situations, and your job is to find three hidden opportunities.

Situation 1: Ten apple trees are growing in your yard, blocking your view of the sunset.

Hidden Opportunities:

1) _____

2) _____

3) _____

Situation 2: The store ran out of your favorite dessert.

Hidden Opportunities:

1) _____

2) _____

3) _____

See how many opportunities you can identify in your everyday life. *Upgrade Your Life* is about being opportunity-minded. An opportunity-minded person sees opportunity everywhere. A defeat-minded person sees defeat everywhere. Your mind does not show you what you want. It shows you the world according to your knowledge. Begin speaking words of opportunities and be fascinated by life. Focus on finding opportunities in everything, and everything will begin to reveal itself as an opportunity.

The way we focus is through words. Situational sight-shifting uses cognitive reframing. In the first exercise, you reframed the problems as opportunities waiting to be found. Sometimes, these opportunities are disguised as something bad. Can you find the good in the bad? Only if you see it. What if you can see the consequences of your actions that are not visible even though those consequences would not happen for another ten years? Would you take action now? Yes!

Sight-shifting is about the power to see and the power to act. It gathers more information to help you take better action. The goal is to practice this exercise with everything and everyone around you. You get so good at it after a few weeks that you won't even have to try anymore because you will begin to realize how life leaves us golden opportunities everywhere. People will be amazed at how you magically have all the answers. To develop this skill mastery, practice it for 30 minutes a day. You will find so many opportunities to develop this skill.

Sight Shifting Exercise 2: Finding the Gap

The purpose of this exercise is to give you control of what you see in yourself. This exercise will develop the skill of seeing the greatness in yourself. First, write down what you see when you see yourself and who you will be in ten years. Give a lot of detail. What would you want everyone to say about that person? The difference between what you would like to see and what you see now is the work you have to do. We call that the "gap". Next, develop a system for filling in that gap. After you complete this book, you will know how to create that system to become the person you have always wanted to be.

1) How do you see the current you?

_____

_____

_____

2) How do you see the future version of yourself?

_____

_____

_____

3) What is the difference between your current and future self?

_____

_____

_____

4) What advice would your future self give to the current you?

_____

_____

Sight Shifting Exercise 3: Headline News

The purpose of this exercise is to help you write your own life story. This exercise will develop the skill to redefine every situation that happens to you at the time it is happening. Words have power over our minds, so names are important. Changing the name of a product, team, or yourself shifts how people see you and things that have the name changed. Words can change what someone sees. In this exercise, we will play a game called "Headline Newstory." Imagine the negative thoughts in your mind as a sad newspaper headline. Now, rewrite the headline to be about something positive. For example, construction workers block the road when you are late. Your original negative headline may be: "I Hate All These Road Blocks These Construction Workers Are Putting Up." The new headline would be: "Construction Workers Helped Me Slow Down and Pay Attention to the Dangers of a Construction Zone." It is all about how you choose to see the world. Now, it's your turn.

Negative Headline: I dropped all the eggs on the floor.

New Positive Headline: _____

_____

Negative Headline: I am not smart enough to do that.

New Positive Headline: _____

_____

Sight Exercise 4: Get Instant Energy

This exercise shows you how to get instant energy when needed and develops the skill of turning challenges into opportunities. Can you find the good in the bad? Can you find the diamond in the sea of rocks? If you can change your words, you can see those opportunities and get the energy and excitement to jumpstart any action. This magic sight is the secret sauce to taking action!

For example, the thought "I have to go to work" can be turned into a power statement by changing the idea to "I get the opportunity to go to work to help provide for my family. I am grateful because some people do not have jobs. And I am using this job to take me towards my goals". Out of nowhere, you will find the strength to go to work because words are power. Like magic, words can give you the energy you need to get through the moment. Small changes in your words make the difference. Change words that have no power into powerful words that support your goals.

There are so many opportunities hidden in our words. Below are actions that may be boring but necessary. These phrases rob you of the power to take action. Next, change the weak phrase into a power phrase and write the new word on the second line in a way that brings out the opportunities.

Ordinary: I need to exercise, but I don't feel like it.

Power Phrase: _____

Ordinary: I feel so lazy.

Power Phrase: _____

Ordinary: It is raining so bad out here.

Power Phrase: _____

Sight Exercise 5: Get More Instant Energy

You will be the one to lead yourself out of sad places when things go wrong in your life. How do you change a pity party into a celebration? You have to open your door to happiness. Sometimes, we are unaware of that happiness when our doors are shut, but better words can help open stubborn doors. In this exercise, take a negative thought about yourself. Don't worry; we all have at least one of these lies we have believed for years. Take one of the words used to describe you in the left column. In the right column, change that word to a positive and more powerful word so the results pull you toward your system actions.

Old Word (The Lie)	New Power Word (The Truth)

There is so much more to sight-shifting. I have another book coming out that teaches this ancient sight-shifting system. However, if you do these exercises daily, you will master the skills needed to become the key to your success, and you can turn problems into profit. In the next chapter, you will develop your *Upgrade Your Life* goal-based system.

CHAPTER NINE

Become a Keymaster: Develop Your Goal-Based System

What you want, you must first become!

The difference between who you are and who you want to be is the system you are building for yourself now. Now that you have goals, powerful reasons, strengths, and sight-shifting skills, it is time to develop your success system. Consider it the price of admission for your better life.

Caution: *This system only works if you have gone through the steps in each chapter of this book. If you have not, take a couple of days to reread the book and complete the steps. Not doing so would be like baking a cake without having all the ingredients to make it rise.*

In this chapter, you will create a goal-based system to *Upgrade Your Life* that is *measurable*. It is a system of becoming the key to your success, the evolutionary step that will help you develop the consistency you need to achieve your goals. This chapter is where you will become a new person; you must allow yourself to become a new person if you want a new life. To have more, you have to become more.

What we have been doing this entire time is having you identify all the parts needed to build your goal-based system. You are setting up your system to develop you into the key to your success. You can have several subsystems running at once. A subsystem is a system within an integrated system that takes you towards a smaller goal. It is important that these subsystems align with each other, and all systems need to align with your goals, beliefs, and values. One subsystem may be to become a healthy eater. Another subsystem may be to learn a new language. The best way to defeat old habits is to develop a subsystem to change that habit. It is much easier to go after a goal than to avoid a problem by becoming the person who can handle it rather than quitting. So, becoming a healthy eater is much easier and more sustainable than stopping an action like eating junk food.

Becoming something means you create a new identity for yourself. After you have become a new person, the old habits will begin to protest and fight against you. Let's look at the food example from the last paragraph. Becoming a healthy person and eating foods that lead to disease creates two worlds that will naturally fight each other. However, you must create a subsystem for eliminating unhealthy food and becoming healthier. Your systems can break your habits if you build a system around the change you want to see. The *Upgrade Your Life* system is designed to help you transform. If you have done the following steps, you will become the person who unlocks the doors of your success.

Your Goal-Based System: The Price You Are Paying for Your Goals

Your system should include a list of tasks you complete every day. Consistency with these tasks will give you so much confidence and trust that you will develop the inner strength of discipline. As you write your system, consider the goals and strengths you created earlier in this book. We are going to use them to give your system unstoppable direction. You may be surprised to see the connections between your strengths and goals, which may be solutions that can solve big problems for a large group of people. Make sure your system has all the elements of a good system: goals and objectives, components, structure, inputs, results, feedback mechanisms, efficiency, effectiveness, reliability, durability, adaptability, and growth.

Name Your New System

Names are a powerful way to commit to anything. By giving something a name, you place it in your environment, making it hard to escape. It is easy to forget someone if you do not know their name. Let's start your new *Upgrade Your Life* goal-based system by naming it. Write the name of your new system on a document or notepad; this will be page one of your new system.

Goal Chart

Next, look back on the goals you made in **Chapter 6**. Write down your goals. You may have a list of 20 goals, and that is great! I gave you room for three goals so you can get started. Next to each goal, write down the goal number for each goal. For small goals, write down "Level 1". For medium-sized goals, write down "Level 2". For big goals, write down "Level 3".

Goal	Goal Level

Qualifying for Your Goals

As you make your goals, you need to know what it takes to be qualified to receive them. If you are missing any qualifications, develop a plan for achieving those qualifications and build those actions into your system. Once you do that, you will know exactly how long it will take to be qualified. Everyone pays a price for their goals. The price you pay is the work you have to do on yourself. The price may be really big. Decide now if you are willing to pay it because, in the immortal words of Jim Rohn, if you think trying is hard, wait till you get the bill for not trying.

Below are three spaces, but use a separate document to list your qualifications for your goals if you need to.

Goal	Qualifications

Strengths Chart

Next, look back on the lists cf strengths you made in Chapter 5 while doing the inventory of yourself. Write down those strengths and skills below and assign them a strength number.

S#	List Strength/Skill

The "S" will be an abbreviation used to represent the strength or skill being used or supported in your system. The number will represent which strength or skill is being used. For example, S2 indicates the second strength or skill on your strength chart.

Reasons Chart

Next, look back on the lists of reasons you made in Chapter 7.

Write down the reason numbers and reason. This chart may have 10-30 reasons, and that is to be expected. You need a powerful list of reasons to get anything done over time.

R#	List Reasons

The "R" will be an abbreviation representing the reason being used or supported in your system. The number will represent which reason is being used. For example, R3 will mean the third reason on your reason chart.

Integrated System

It is time to write your integrated system. These are the smaller systems that tie your whole life together. They are the internal organs of your system that pump life-giving blood to your dreams.

Creating an integrated system may seem like hard work, and it is. I will not try to convince you any differently, but that is why most people don't do it. Make sure you are not one of those people. Commit to designing your life so you can reach your goals.

This section will separate your system into daily actions and weekly check-ins. These are going to be the actions that will take you towards your goals. In school, teachers call these course objectives. Your life is now a series of systems until you reach your goal. You must find solutions to problems holding you back and use a system to fix them. For everything you need to do, build a system around it. Start by creating a system that develops you into the person who deserves the goals you want. You may use another person's system if that system will take you forward. You can use someone else's system to help build yours by finding your goal and researching other people who have achieved that goal. Look at the hard work and daily disciplines in their lives. Use this information to help build your system.

Let's get started! We will begin by having you complete a Goal-to-Action chart. This chart is a snapshot of your goals and everything you need to complete those goals. My advice is to start by creating a system that solves problems in your life. Next, develop systems for what you want in life. Then, develop systems that solve problems for other people. On the first line, write one of your goals. Next, write the goal level for that particular goal. Below, write all the actions that will take you towards that goal. On the following line, indicate how well each action supports the goal. On a scale from 1-10, how strongly does that habit support your goal? Revise the action until the score is at least an 8 out of 10.

On the following line, write down how long it will take you to do that action. Most of these actions should be done daily for consistency, and consistency is a major key to your better future. On the following line, circle whether this action is completed daily, weekly, or monthly. Next, write down when you will do that action. Next, write down the strength number the action supports. On the last line, write down the reason number the action supports. List the daily actions (habits) you will commit to for each goal. Include actions to support your daily life and what you value in life. Include actions to support the following systems: physical health, mental health, relationships, family, finances, goals, and any other valuable parts of your life.

Goal-to-Action Chart

Goal 1:_____

Goal Level: _____

Actions: _____

Action to Goal Support Level (1-10): _____

Time to Complete Action:_____

Action Is Completed: (Circle)   Daily   Weekly   Monthly

What Time of Day?: _____

Strength Number Supported:_____

Reason Number: _____

Write your bottom-line statement. (Your bottom line is the line you reach when you need to panic because you have not reached your goal.)

_____

_____

Goal-to-Action Chart

Goal 2:_____

Goal Level: _____

Actions: _____

Action to Goal Support Level (1-10): _____

Time to Complete Action:_____

Action Is Completed: (Circle) Daily Weekly Monthly

What Time of Day?: _____

Strength Number Supported:_____

Reason Number: _____

Write your bottom-line statement for this goal. (Reminder: Your bottom line is the line you reach when you need to panic because you have not reached your goals.)

_____

_____

Goal-to-Action Chart

Goal 3:_____

Goal Level: _____

Actions: _____

Action to Goal Support Level (1-10): _____

Time to Complete Action:_____

Action Is Completed: (Circle)   Daily   Weekly   Monthly

What Time of Day?: _____

Strength Number Supported:_____

Reason Number: _____

Write your bottom-line statement for this goal. (Reminder: Your bottom line is the line you reach when you need to panic because you have not reached your goals.)

_____

_____

Write a Goal-to-Action chart for each of your goals. You are now excelling in the School of Life, and your job is developing your goals, objectives, lesson plans, and homework. Life will give you the test before the lesson, and then it will graduate and elevate you to the next grade. And sometimes, the test is the lesson. Once you have this information, you know your daily actions are taking you toward your goals because your actions will be in line with your goals. You will be able to draw a straight line to your goals. The straighter the line, the more direction you have in life.

Integrated Systems Action Schedule Checklist

Now that you have written down your actions, transfer those actions to a checklist. The goal is to check off every action at the end of the day. Your lists may have 20-50 actions a day. That is very normal. In the first column marked **Action**, write the action. In the second column marked **Completion**, write day and time you completed each action. Spread these actions out across your day. Some actions are better done in the morning, while others are better completed at night.

Action	Completion Day/Time

Systems keep you on track. Throughout your journey, your feelings will try to take over and slow down your progress. Sometimes, you will not feel like doing anything but relaxing, and it is also okay to rest. You will need it. However, work hard to get your best average to 90% so you can at least get an A in the School of Life. If you have to, you can settle for a B. But never settle for a C, and know if you get below a C, you are failing yourself. Get an A in the School of Life and get the rewards!

Review and Revise

Review your checklist at the end of the day. Find areas of improvement. Some actions need to be improved, added, or eliminated. Take time to revise your checklist when needed. Look for balance. Are some activities being completed more than others? Are some goals being completed more than others? It is time to commit to completing all the actions on your list or revise it to have actions you can complete. I caution you not to take the easy route. If you do what is easy, life will be hard. But if you do what is hard, life will be easy.

As you grow in life, this system will need to be revised. If you do not need to modify your system, that is a red flag that you are not growing and need to adjust your system. The bottom line is that you will always need to adapt your system because either life is changing or you are. And if life is changing, you better take the time to adjust to it. The most successful companies that have failed usually fail because they refuse to change their systems. They say things like, "This is the way we have always done it," and life responds by saying, "Your reward is failure, just as it has always been done throughout history." The revision will help you reach your goals faster.

Scoring

Start giving yourself a daily score to measure your progress. You want to score in the top 10% because you want a top 10% life. To find out your score, we have to do a little math. Add up all of your daily activities. Take the total number of actions you completed and divide them by the total number of actions on the list. Next, move the decimal point to the right by two numbers and add a percent (%) sign. That is your score for the day. Here is an example.

- Let's say you completed 14 of the 20 actions for the day.

- Divide 14 by 20. The answer is .70. Then move the decimal point to the right twice, and your score will be 70%. This score is the same as getting 70% on a homework assignment, a grade of **C**.

- Tomorrow, the goal should be to raise your score to at least 90% so you can score an **A** in the School of Life.

Finding Your Monthly Average

You can quickly measure your progress toward your goals. At the end of 30 days, take all your scores, add them up, and divide them by 30. That is your monthly score. Do this every month and strive to get an A in the School of Life. When you have a high score, you will be guaranteed to reach your goals!

Assignment: Draw a straight line from your goals to success. If things on the list don't line up, you have some cleaning to do. Below are the areas that must always be in alignment.

Goals + Reasons + Systems + Mindset + Time = Success

The Mirror - Beginning Your Day

- Say out loud the best version of what you see.

- Tell yourself what you are grateful for.

- Then, write down your action steps for the day based on the best version of you.

- Silent Seminar - program your phone to give you wisdom messages throughout your day, especially starting your day.

Five-Step Daily Reflection

At the end of the day, read over your system and determine how well you did.

- Daily News Headlines: It is time to learn from the day. Write down the major events of the day. These are your opportunities and challenges. There is an opportunity to learn from every event. If you do not see an opportunity, shift your sight of the event and find the opportunity. You should be able to write a story about the opportunities for the day's event.

- Celebrate Goals: Celebrate every time you reach a goal or have success! If you did well, then congratulate yourself. It may not be every day, but when they come, celebrate.

- Action Checklist: Write your actions for the next day. For each action, write down how each action supports your goals.

- The Scale: On a scale from 1 to 10, how strongly does that action support your goal? Revise and upgrade each action until your score is at least an 8 out of 10.

- System Upgrade: Review your system weekly, monthly, and yearly.

Review your goals every day and update them every week. This system is the price you pay for your goals. What happens if your system isn't working? Remember, the prize comes at the end of any race, not the beginning. Stay consistent and work your system. All systems work.

Systems can either be programmed with intentional goals or spin out of control and produce random goals. The system has no sense of right or wrong. It is like a car or a plane. It will go wherever your daily actions tell it to go. You will have to study your system to know what goals it is producing. If your system is taking you away from your goals, stop and revise your system. Either way you look at it, building and running your system is hard work. Laziness pays off now, but hard work pays off in the future. Put in the hard work and get the good results in your life.

Here is a tip on accountability. Inspect what you expect from your systems. If you do not complete your daily actions, how will you make up for it? You need to balance the books every day by accounting for all habits. Also, do any daily actions violate your values or beliefs? If they do, eliminate those actions and develop actions that align with your values and beliefs. Can each action be done consistently daily? If not, then revise the action until you can perform it consistently. Like any school, you will have homework. The daily actions are your homework assignments. However, you must become a teacher by creating and grading your own homework. This system is the plan you are writing to advance you to the next grade level. The teacher is now staring at you in the mirror. You are responsible for your education now.

Measure the Gap

The gap is the distance you are away from reaching your goal. Knowing the gap will help you upgrade your system and prevent discouragement, as achieving your goals might take longer than planned. However, the gap can only be measured over time. To do this, we need to gather all the **Daily News Headlines** you have written at the end of every day for the past month.

Step 1: At the end of the month, make a numbered list of your Daily News Headlines.

Step 2: Finding the Gap

- If you read your list from beginning to end, your headlines will read like a story. Now ask yourself this:

- Does your story this month sound like it will lead to your goals? How can you adjust your daily actions to tell a better story if not?

- After reviewing your stories from the past six months, does this month's story sound like it will lead to my goals? If not, how can I adjust my monthly stories to have a better story? Those adjusted stories can help you restructure your daily actions.

Step 3: Measuring the Gap

- The distance between where you are and your goals is "The Gap".

- Based on my story, how long would it take me to reach my goals?

- Only you can answer this question. It takes serious thinking, but after reviewing the past six months, you can find your gap.

Maintaining Mental Sight Health

Now that you have developed your system, it is time to take action. Think about a powerful reason to take action on your integrated system; this is the secret sauce that will keep you on task. Read your reasons daily and memorize them. Then, when you need motivation and inspiration, just pull out your list of reasons to give you a jumpstart. By having your powerful list of reasons, you will never run out of reasons to take action. Most people have problems because they run out of reasons as soon as the excitement wears off. However, you will get excited over your ability to make yourself take the necessary actions to *Upgrade Your Life* because you have an unstoppable list of reasons.

Over time, this daily system becomes your daily habit. Systems become habits you don't have to think about anymore. Your system will go on autopilot. You will find yourself taking action toward your goals without even working hard because you have done the hard work of developing your mind, defining your goals, developing your reasons, growing your sight, and creating actions that will take you toward your goals. You did not sit around and hope things would happen. You developed a system for making things happen! Soon, you will rise to a new level in life, just like a cake rises when baked. You put in the right ingredients and took out the wrong ingredients by designing a fantastic system. McDonald's doesn't sell billions more than small hamburger places because they have better hamburgers. They sell more because they have a tremendous system to sell happiness in a box with a toy. Now, you have a system to reach your goals in life. It is your system that will take you to your goals. Use reasons to give you the energy and emotions to go after your system daily.

Raising Your Score: How to Raise Your Commitment Level

Going to new levels means setting new goals, reevaluating your current sight level, and tailoring your system. For new levels, you will need to find new reasons and evaluate the strength of those reasons. Go back to your reasons scores from Chapter 7 and revise your list. You are ready to start when your number is over 70%. When your reason score is over 90%, then you are nearly unstoppable.

You will experience period of mental conditioning to accept the new system. For several months, your brain will try to return to its default mode, old programming. You must reinforce your new system every day until it becomes a part of who you are. The gap between who you are and who you want to be is the system you have built for yourself using *Upgrade Your Life*. Know that when you better yourself, you must allow time for everything else to catch up. Time makes the difference. So congratulations! You have taken the time, made the difference, and begun to *Upgrade Your Life*!

CHAPTER TEN

You Are Now the Unstoppable Key!

First become the key and then open the door. (Lorne Lee)

You are now prepared with everything you need to become the unstoppable key to the door of your goals. You have taken control of the automatic system you were born with and developed it into a goal-based system that will shape you into the key that opens the door to your goals. As you work on your daily system, think about the big picture at least once a month. The big picture is the success you will see when you add all your goals together. The **Upgrade Your Life** system is about becoming the unstoppable master key that opens all doors. Master keys are special keys. In a building, everyone may have a specific key to their office, but a master key unlocks every door in the building. That is why becoming a master key is so powerful.

Keep asking questions. Better question skills lead to better answers and a better life. Myron Golden says, "I would rather have questions that I cannot answer rather than answers that I cannot question." What in your life are you not questioning? If you want something you can't see with your natural eyes in the future, you have to decide to be the person inside who sees beyond the present.

How do you find the right doors? Does that door align with your goals? Test those doors because some doors should be avoided. How do you protect your key? Your key does not work on broken locks. Your key will not work in a door it was not designed to open. But a master key opens all doors, good and bad. You are becoming the master key that will open the doors to your success. When you find the right doors and develop into the right key, you can become the key that opens multiple doors.

How Do You Keep Up Momentum Every Day?

Momentum has been designed into your system by using discipline to maintain consistency and your powerful list of reasons to give you the drive you need. All of this is part of the *Upgrade Your Life* system design. As your momentum builds, your consistency will build. You will find yourself feeling incomplete if you do not carry out your system every day. That feeling lets you know the system is becoming automatic, so you do not have to concentrate on it.

Momentum is like using cruise control on a car. You just run the system and cruise toward your goals. You will develop more discipline as you work your system, and the consistency of discipline plus powerful reasons are the keys to momentum. Go back through your *Upgrade Your Life* system and see if momentum is built in to be automatic. Adjust your daily actions to make your system more powerful and automatic. Whatever you want out of life, make it a study, and then make it a system. Don't leave it to chance. Make it a system.

Exercise: Creating a Quick System

Your ability to quickly create systems is another key to success in the *Upgrade Your Life* system. Quick systems are ones that you make to handle everyday situations. When I was in grad school, I used to take the bus across the country. One time, I was stuck in a busy bus station. I waited for the buses for hours. There were so many lines of people, and everyone also had their luggage with them. As the hundreds of travelers walked through the crowded bus station, they kept cutting through our line and knocking our luggage over as they tried to leap over the bags. The people in my line were getting frustrated. I saw an opportunity to help, so I found a solution to the problem.

I said, "Hey everyone. I know you are tired of people cutting through our line. I have a solution. I bet we can control this whole bus station by creating a system all other travelers in the bus station would follow. Are you interested?" Everyone was interested in having their problems go away. "Ok. We will create a three-foot gap in our line for every five people. We will have four gaps in total. When people see the path of least resistance we create, I bet you they will take it."

Next, my line created the gaps, and every traveler in the bus station traveled through the gaps we made. No one in the bus station got upset because there were only four gaps to travel through. My theory was that everyone takes the path of least resistance, and it worked. I built a quick system to handle a problem in my everyday life that had nothing to do with my goals but everything to do with the person I was becoming. I quickly created a system that helped 50 people in an overcrowded bus station during wintertime. You will have opportunities to develop systems to handle everyday challenges. Your ability to create quick systems will accelerate your success journey.

Being Qualified to Receive Your Goals

Either you are qualified, or you get qualified. Those are your only two options if you want your goals. And how do you know that you are qualified? When the key can open the door. Until your key opens the door, keep developing yourself through the system you created. We will list the standard qualifications here. When you can answer yes to these questions, you are qualified.

- I have studied what I want.

- I can identify the type of person who qualifies for that position.

- I have studied what it took for them to reach my goals.

- I have built a system incorporating what it takes to reach my goals and studied the right mindset.

- I have developed a powerful list of reasons for reaching my goals.

- I know my strengths and weaknesses and have developed a system for improving my weaknesses.

- I have learned how to shift my sight.

- I have taken action on my system with consistency and commitment over time. (This could take one to ten years.)

Those are the qualifications. If you change a little to move towards it, your life will get better a little. If you change massively, your life will get better massively. The more you move towards your goal, the better your life will be And the only reason your life will get better is because you are getting better. When you are better, everything will get better. It is time to be better.

A Game of Hide and Seek

You will play a game of hide and seek for the rest of your life because answers hide from you until you have the right questions. When that question comes, the answers will jump out at you. If that is the game, then use the rules to your advantage. Became a master at finding the right questions. Change your question if you are not getting the correct answers or understanding the answer. When questions change, the answers change. Learning to ask the right questions is a skill. Whether you are a firefighter, an FBI agent, or a doctor, asking the right questions could be life or death. So, they are trained in the art of asking the right questions. When you do not ask the right questions, things do not go well, but you can save lives if you ask the right questions. You do not have to have all the answers in life. Get into the School of Life and learn how to ask the right questions because the world opens up for people with the right questions.

How to Attract Success

How do you attract quality people? You do this by becoming more attractive. I do not mean being physically more attractive; becoming more attractive means raising your level to attract people on your new level. If you want to attract higher-level people, raise your level.

When you become the unstoppable key, all doors will become visible, waiting to be opened. It's almost like magic. The doors are looking for keys because they want to be opened, and those are looking for you! The next part of attracting success is the principle that says you find yourself everywhere; this is a difficult concept for some to accept.

The reason you must become a better person is so you can attract better people. The reason some hotels cost $100 a night and other hotels cost $10,000 a night is that the hotels are attracting different people. The reason there are games and toys at McDonald's is because they are attracting kids. Everyone is attracting who they want, whether they know it or not. So, join the top achievers of life by becoming aware of what and who you are attracting. If you think this way, the doors of your goals will come to you much faster. They will not appear open, but the unstoppable key you have become will allow you to open those doors.

Remember, all systems are perfect. They will give out the finished product of all the ingredients and instructions you put in. So, if you do not like what the system is producing, check the system and check the ingredients. If all that is good, check the user for operator error (**Pro tip: You are the operator.**). Your system has to be designed so well that even if you change your mind about what you want to do, your system will still work as designed. To change your goals, you need to overhaul your system.

Let's take a closer look. You were a baby, and now you have grown into an adult. You have witnessed a fantastic system that works. Life grows like a tree, and like a tree, you will never see growth in the moment. Growth is a measurement seen over time. A tree grows in time, just like you will. The tree doesn't have to think about how to be successful; it was born into a system set up for success. Ants worldwide have a successful system of creating tunnels that work every time. It is not magic; it is a system, and with the right system, success is automatic. Allow time for your system to work. If you have the right system and give it time, success will be automatic.

Next, start your system, and don't stop. Every day, keep going, and don't stop. In reality, you are the only one who can stop your progress. If you decide to be committed to the system and carry it out repeatedly every day, no one can stop you except the person in the mirror. With all the reasons in the world to keep you going, you won't stop. And that is how you become the unstoppable key. Follow the system you created in this book and become the **unstoppable key** to your success, and then become the big solution to a large group of people's big needs.

Conclusion

You have now upgraded your life. You have followed the *Upgrade Your Life* system to build a system that shapes you into the key to your success, shaped by daily actions aligned with your goals. You have been given the most powerful tool in the world, the power to shape yourself into who you know you need to be. You are the key that will unlock the doors to your goal. It will take time, but growth is measured over time.

You cannot see a person grow any more than you can watch a flower grow. You can only see growth over time and measure it against where you used to be. Don't look to see growth in yourself daily. Look to be consistent and measure your growth over time. Remember, the goal is to become the right key to the doors you want to open. And how do you know you have become the right key? You will see the key when you look in the mirror, and you will trust it as it opens doors for you. When you work hard on your system, the results are automatic. After you have made your system, re-read *Upgrade Your Life* to revise your system. If you did not write your system the first time you read the book, then re-read this book and write your system as you go along. And remember the formula for success with your system:

Goals + Reasons + Systems + Mindset + Time = Success

Don't look for your dreams to come true. Look to become the key that unlocks your dreams, and then, you can become the key that unlocks other people's dreams. If you want to help your family and friends change their lives, have them read *Upgrade Your Life*. What you want, you must first become. When you become the unstoppable key to your success, you will have the power to open the door to all your goals and dreams.

Reading List for Success

Every successful person I know has a reading list of the books that have shaped their lives. When I found out what successful people were reading, I read those books. Those books changed my life. Now, I will share my reading list with you.

Top 14 Books and Why I Read Them

1. Emotional Intelligence (by Daniel Goleman)

   - Why: This book helped me understand and manage my emotions, improve relationships, and achieve tremendous success by teaching me how to use my emotions effectively.

2. Good to Great (by James C. Collins)

   - Why: This book helped me understand why some companies and people become successful and others don't.

3. How to Win Friends and Influence People (by Dale Carnegie)

   - Why: This book helped me understand how to create strong relationships and improve my communication skills.

4. Rich Dad Poor Dad (by Robert Kiyosaki)

   - Why: This book helped me understand how money works by teaching me the lessons rich people teach their kids that the rest of us did not get growing up.

5. Richest Man in Babylon (by George Samuel Clason)

   - Why? This book taught me about saving, investing, and budgeting.

6. 7 Habits of Highly Successful People (by Stephen Covey)

- Why? This book gave helpful steps to help me manage my life and work with others.

7. The Alchemist (by Paulo Coelho)

- Why: This book helped me understand the importance of finding meaning and purpose in my life journey. It encouraged me to embrace challenges and live in the present moment.

8. The Five Love Languages (by Gary Chapman)

- Why? This book helped me understand how others receive me and how I want to be received.

9. The Inner Game of Tennis (by Timothy Gallwey)

- Why? This book helped me understand how to overcome self-doubt, nervousness, and lapses in concentration to achieve peak performance in life.

10. The Instant Millionaire (by Mark Fisher)

- Why? This book helped me understand the millionaire mindset and gave me practical advice for achieving financial success.

11. The Truth about Lying (by Stan B. Walters)

- Why? This book gave me skills that can help me spot lies. It helped me tell the difference between what is true and what is not, both in my everyday life and at work.

12. Think & Grow Rich (by Napolean Hill)

- Why? This book helped me understand how to reach my goals for money and happiness. The book taught important ideas on goal-setting and developing a winner's mindset.

13. Unlimited Power (by Anthony Robbins)

- Why? This book helped me understand how to transform my life by unlocking my inner potential through the science of personal achievement.

14. Who Moved My Cheese? (by Spencer Johnson)

- Why? This book taught me how to adjust quickly to change and discover new opportunities with flexible thinking.

Read these books if you want to see your life move ahead quicker than others. You will thank me later. Next, develop a reading list about the goals you have set for yourself and the people who have reached those goals. Learn their stories because they often have helpful tips that could save you five or ten years of going in the wrong direction. This study will help you design an even more powerful system.

References

Abbott, T. M., Aguena, M., Alarcon, A., Allam, S., Alves, O., Amon, A., & Smith, M. (2022). Dark Energy Survey Year 3 results: Cosmological constraints from galaxy clustering and weak lensing. *Physical Review D, 105*(2), 023520.

Aversa, P., Haefliger, S., Hueller, F., & Reza, D. G. (2021). Customer complementarity in the digital space: Exploring Amazon's business model diversification. *Long Range Planning, 54*(5). https://doi-org.occc.idm.oclc.org/10.1016/j.lrp.2020.101985

Baard, S. K., Rench, T. A., &; Kozlowski, S. W. (2014). Performance adaptation: A theoretical integration and review. *Journal of Management, 40*(1), 48-99.

Bolman, L. G., & Deal, T. E. (1991). *Reframing organizations: Artistry, choice, and leadership.* Jossey-Bass/Wiley.

Campbell, J. (2014). *The hero's journey.* New World Library.

Chen, M., Guo, L., Ramakrishnan, M., Fei, Z., Vinod, K., Ding, Y., Jiao, C., Gao, Z., Zha, R., Wang, C., Gao, Z., Yu, F., Ren, G., Wei, Q. (2022). Rapid growth of Moso bamboo (Phyllostachys edulis): Cellular roadmaps, transcriptome dynamics, and environmental factors. *The Plant Cell, 34*(10), 3577–3610. https://doi.org/10.1093/plcell/koac193

Daughterty, G. (2023, October 2) The rise and fall of telephone operators. *History Channel.* https://www.history.com/news/rise-fall-telephone-switchboard-operators

Dittfurth, E., Joiner, S., & Heller, J. A. (2024). Mcdonald's Franchise - Steal the King. *Journal of Business & Educational Leadership, 14*(1), 61–73.

Gerber, M. E. (1995). *The E-myth revisited: why most small businesses don't work and what to do about it.* New York, N.Y., Collins Business.

Glück, J. (2018). Measuring wisdom: Existing approaches, continuing challenges, and new developments. *The Journals of Gerontology: Series B, 73*(8), 1393-1403.

Hassel, A., & Sieker, F. (2022). The platform effect: How Amazon changed work in logistics in Germany, the United States and the United Kingdom. *European Journal of Industrial Relations, 28*(3), 363–382. https://doi-org.occc.idm.oclc.org/10.1177/09596801221082456

Lechêne, Robert (2024, June 4). History of printing. *Encyclopedia Britannica.* https://www.britannica.com/topic/printing-publishing. Accessed August 27, 2024.

Levy, J. S. (1998). The causes of war and the conditions of peace. *Annual Review of Political Science, 1*(1), 139-165.

LoBue, V., & Adolph, K. E. (2019). Fear in infancy: Lessons from snakes, spiders, heights, and strangers. *Dev Psychol., 55*(9), 1889-1907. doi:10.1037/dev0000675.PMID:31464493; PMCID: PMC6716607.

Magliano, J. P., Kopp, K., Higgs, K,, & Rapp, D. N. (2017). Filling in the gaps: Memory implications for inferring missing content in graphic narratives. *Discourse Processes, 54,* 569–582. doi: 10.1080/0163853X.2015.1136870.

Mayr, S., Mitter, C.,Kücher, A.; Duller, C. (2021). Entrepreneur characteristics and differences in reasons for business failure: evidence from bankrupt Austrian SMEs. *Journal of Small Business & Entrepreneurship, 33*(5), 539-558.

Milner, P. (2003). A brief history of the Hebbian learning rule. *Canadian Psychology, 44*(1), 5.

Moaveni, S. & Chou, K. (2017). Using the Five Whys Methods in the classroom: How to turn students into Problem Solvers. *Journal of STEM Education, 17*(4). https://www.learntechlib.org/p/174416/.

Noorman, S., Neville, D.A. & Simanova, I. (2018). Words affect visual perception by activating object shape representations. *Sci Rep, 8*, 14156. https://doi.org/10.1038/s41598-018-32483-2

O'Connor, M. C., & Paunonen, S. V. (2007). Big Five personality predictors of post-secondary academic performance. *Personality and Individual Differences, 43(*5), 971-990.

Papenmeier, F., Brockhoff, A., & Huff, M. (2019). Filling the gap despite full attention: The role of fast backward inferences for event completion. *Cognitive Research: Principles and Implications, 4*(1), 3. https://doi.org/10.1186/s41235-018-0151-2

Rohde, M., Di Luca, M., & Ernst, M. O. (2011). The Rubber Hand Illusion: Feeling of ownership and proprioceptive drift do not go hand in hand. *PloS one, 6*(6), e21659. https://doi.org/10.1371/journal.pone.0021659

Schattenburg, M. L. (2007, March 8). History of the "Three Beams" Conference, the Birth of the Information Age and the Era of Lithography Wars. *In International Confer-ence on Electron, Ion, and Photon Beam Technology and Nanofabrication.* Accessed August 27, 2024.

Sharma, A., Rushton, K., Lin, I. W., Wadden, D., Lucas, K. G., Miner, A. S., & Althoff, T. (2023). Cognitive reframing of negative thoughts through human-language model interaction. *In Proceedings of the 61st Annual Meeting of the Association for Computational Linguistics (Volume 1: Long Papers)* pages 9977–10000, Toronto, Canada. *Association for Computational Linguistics.*

Singh, V. A., Kumar, V. G., Banerjee, D. A., & Roy, D. D. (2024). Prestimulus periodic and aperiodic neural activity shapes McGurk perception. *In Proceedings of the Annual Meeting of the Cognitive Science Society, 46.*

Steinwart, M. C., & Ziegler, J. A. (2014). Remembering Apple CEO Steve Jobs as a "Transformational Leader": Implications for Pedagogy. *Journal of Leadership Education, 13*(2), 52–66.

Tuomainen, U., & Candolin, U. (2011). Behavioural responses to human induced environmental change. *Biological Reviews, 86*(3), 640-657.

U.S. Bureau of Labor Statistics (2024). Table 7. Survival of private sector establishments by opening year. https://www.bls.gov/bdm/us_age_naics_00_table7.txt